MILLIONAIRE
TUTOR

ESCAPE YOUR SOUL-CRUSHING 9-TO-5 BY BUILDING AN OUTRAGEOUSLY PROFITABLE TUTORING BUSINESS!

MICHAEL BLACK

First published in 2025 by Success Publishing House

© Success Publishing House 2025
The moral rights of the author have been asserted

All rights reserved. Except as permitted under the *Australian Copyright Act 1968* (for example, a fair dealing for the purposes of study, research, criticism or review), no part of this book may be reproduced, stored in a retrieval system, communicated or transmitted in any form or by any means without prior written permission. No part of this book may be used or reproduced in any manner for the purpose of training artificial intelligence technologies or systems.

All inquiries should be made to info@successpublishinghouse.com

A catalogue entry for this book is available from the National Library of Australia.

ISBN: 978-1-923225-89-3

Cover design by Pipeline Design

The paper this book is printed on is certified as environmentally friendly.

Disclaimer
The material in this publication is of the nature of general comment only, and does not represent professional advice. It is not intended to provide specific guidance for particular circumstances and it should not be relied on as the basis for any decision to take action or not take action on any matter which it covers. Readers should obtain professional advice where appropriate, before making any such decision. To the maximum extent permitted by law, the author and publisher disclaim all responsibility and liability to any person, arising directly or indirectly from any person taking or not taking action based on the information in this publication.

This book is dedicated to my mother, father and sister, who all show me what unconditional love means.

CONTENTS

START HERE
1. Who this book IS NOT for!   1
2. Who is Michael Black?   6

PART 1: THE JOURNEY OF SUCCESS TUTORING
3. History of Success Tutoring   15
4. Why do people get tutoring wrong?   23
5. The philosophy behind Success Tutoring   32
6. Building the McDonald's of tutoring   43
7. The SuccessAcademy (University of Michael Black)   49

PART 2: MINDSET & EXECUTION
8. Ideas are worthless without execution   63
9. Politics is cancer   78
10. Poverty is a mindset   84
11. Have the right mindset   93
12. Everything you know about business is wrong   106
13. Finding your passion   112

PART 3: BUSINESS STRATEGIES & GROWTH
14. The secret sauce to success   125
15. Location, location, location   133
16. Selling franchises like hotcakes   139
17. How to run a really successful tutoring business   144
18. Buying a franchise can change your life   155

PART 4: INDUSTRY INSIGHTS
19. What the government will not tell you   167
20. The broken education system – tutoring is not the solution   173

PART 5: EXPERT ADVICE
21. Tips for parents   183
22. Tips for potential franchise partners   192
23. Tips for aspiring franchisors   203
24. 10 years of knowledge in one chapter   210

CHAPTER 1

WHO THIS BOOK *IS NOT* FOR!

"He who has ears, let him hear."

If you've picked up this book, there's a reason. Something inside of you is searching for more. You're not content with a mediocre life, and you know deep down that you deserve to live bigger, brighter, and bolder. But before we go any further, I need to make something very clear: this book is NOT for everyone.

In fact, I'll go a step further. This book isn't for most people.

This book is not for you if you're perfectly happy with the status quo. It's not for you if you're content working the same 9-to-5 job every day, showing up to a place that doesn't challenge or excite you, counting the hours until Friday and dreading Monday mornings. It's not for you if you're happy trading time for money – year after year, knowing deep down that there's something more out there, but choosing not to chase it. If that's where you are in life, this book might feel uncomfortable.

And maybe that's a good thing.

This book is also not for people who think success is reserved for "other people" – those who are lucky or born into it. If you've convinced yourself that greatness isn't for you or that being wealthy and successful is something to be ashamed of, stop reading now. I can't help you until you're ready to change that mindset.

Let me be blunt: if you believe that living an average life – one income, one holiday a year, working until you're 65 just to retire and *maybe* enjoy a few good years – is all that life has to offer, then this book will challenge everything you think you know. And that might make you uncomfortable. But discomfort is the first step to growth. It's the sign that you're standing on the edge of something bigger, something life-changing.

WHO IS THIS BOOK FOR?

So, who am I writing this for? I'm writing this book for people who want more from life. The people who wake up and say, "I am meant for more." If you're the kind of person who looks at your current situation and feels deep down that you're capable of more – more freedom, more security, more impact – then this book is your guide.

I'm talking to those who are done playing small. You don't want to spend your whole life following someone else's script. You have dreams of running your own business, of being your own boss, of living life on your terms. But here's the kicker: this book is for those who are ready to do the work. Because success doesn't just land in your lap. It's something you have to work for, fight for, and, most importantly, *believe* you deserve.

I've met too many people in my life who have all the potential in the world, but they squander it because they're afraid. Afraid of failure, afraid of success, afraid of what others will think. They settle for less because it's easier than pushing themselves to achieve more. But I'll tell you this: the people who achieve greatness in this life are the ones who refuse to settle.

Do you want a comfortable life? Great, but that's not what this book is about.

This book is about freedom. Freedom to choose how you spend your time, who you spend it with, and what your legacy will be. It's about building a business that not only provides financial security but also gives you the flexibility to live life on your own terms.

FRANCHISING: THE GATEWAY TO MORE

You might be wondering why this book is focused on franchising. Why franchising, and more specifically, why tutoring?

Simple: franchising is the gateway to creating a scalable business model without having to reinvent the wheel. The systems, the processes, the brand – it's already built. All you need is the vision and the drive to make it successful. But not everyone is cut out to be a franchise owner. And that's okay.

I'll tell you right now, if you're looking for an easy way out, this book isn't for you. I'm not offering a get-rich-quick scheme. Success, in franchising or any business, takes commitment, resilience, and the willingness to learn. But here's the good news: the hard part – the foundation – is already built. The Success Tutoring model has been proven time and time again. It works. All you have to do is plug into the system and commit to making it thrive.

But you need passion. You need to believe in what we do. At Success Tutoring, we're not just teaching students; we're changing lives. We motivate, inspire, and uplift students to reach their full potential. If that doesn't light a fire in you – if you're just here to make a quick buck – then you're in the wrong place.

Let me be clear: franchising is about consistency. It's about systems. It's about ensuring that every franchise follows the same winning formula that has already been laid out. I didn't create Success Tutoring by accident. It was built with intention, with a vision for excellence, and with a passion for impacting lives through education.

A LIFE OF ABUNDANCE

Here's the thing about success: it's not just about the money. Yes, financial freedom is important, but that's not the end goal. Success is about living a life of abundance. And when I say abundance, I'm talking about abundance in all areas of life – time, energy, relationships, and yes, finances.

If you're happy living in scarcity – scraping by on one income, taking one holiday a year, and calling that a life – then this book is going to feel like a punch in the gut. But sometimes we need that punch to wake us up.

Success Tutoring isn't just a business. It's a vehicle for freedom. I built it from the ground up, and today it's one of the fastest-growing education franchises in the world. With locations in Australia and New Zealand, we are now expanding into the United Kingdom, Singapore, Canada and the United States – and we're just getting started. Why? Because the model works. And if you're the right person, it can work for you too.

But you have to want it.

You have to want more for yourself, your family, and your future. And if that's you, then this book is going to change your life.

A WORD ON MINDSET

Now, let's talk about mindset. You've probably heard it before, but let me tell you straight up: mindset is everything. If you don't believe that you're capable of achieving more, then you won't. If you don't believe that you deserve success, you'll never have it. I'm not here to sugarcoat anything – success is a mental game. And the people who win are the ones who refuse to let limiting beliefs control their lives.

I've seen it time and time again – people with all the talent, all the resources, and yet they fall short because they don't have the right mindset. They're too afraid to fail, or they're too comfortable in their current situation to take the risk. But let me tell you something: *everything in life is risky*. Staying in your comfort zone is risky. Playing small is risky. And the biggest risk of all is waking up one day and realising you never truly lived.

So, I'm going to ask you again: are you ready to break free from mediocrity? Are you ready to build something that matters? Because if you are, then you've come to the right place.

IS THIS BOOK FOR YOU?

At the end of this chapter, you should have a pretty clear idea of whether this book is for you. If you're happy with average, this book won't serve you. But if you're hungry for more – more freedom, more success, more fulfilment – then buckle up. You're about to embark on a journey that has the potential to change everything.

The principles in this book aren't just about running a tutoring business. They're about building a life of purpose, passion, and abundance. They're about stepping into your highest potential and creating a legacy that will outlast you.

So, let me leave you with this: *he who has ears, let him hear.* If you're ready to hear, to learn, and to grow – if you're open to the possibilities that await you – then this book is for you.

CHAPTER 2

WHO IS MICHAEL BLACK?

Who am I, and why am I telling you this story? These are the two most important questions you should be asking yourself as you turn these pages. You might wonder what qualifies me to offer guidance, insight, or advice in a world brimming with "how-to" books and motivational content. The truth is, my qualifications come not from titles or certifications but from a lifetime of lived experience. From humble beginnings, I developed a burning passion for business and a deep belief in the power of personal motivation. So, let me take you back to where it all began.

I was born and raised in a suburb called Bossley Park in Sydney's western suburbs, about 50 kilometres away from the Central Business District (CBD). It wasn't an area where dreams of grandeur or billion-dollar business empires were commonplace, but from a young age, I was always different. I was fascinated by big business and driven by a sense that I was meant for something greater than my immediate surroundings.

LEARNING FROM FAMILY

Growing up, I had countless conversations with my dad about his work. My father, Fayez, worked in corporate life, specifically in sourcing, logistics, and supply chain. His area of expertise was negotiating deals with large suppliers for massive corporations, including industry giants like Wesfarmers – a company you've probably heard of as a blue-chip business. Watching my father navigate the complexities of operations and deal-making sparked a fire in me. I wasn't just curious; I was captivated. I wanted to know everything about how businesses worked, how deals were made, and how people could take an idea and turn it into something impactful.

That early exposure to the corporate world gave me a broad understanding of how things operated behind the scenes. My dad would talk to me about organisational structure, operational processes, and the importance of consistency and quality. He was a conservative man when it came to business; he preferred the safety of a steady paycheck. There's nothing wrong with that mindset, but even as a child, I knew that wasn't the path I wanted to follow. I respected my dad immensely, but I had a burning desire for something riskier, more adventurous – something that could change my life and the lives of others.

On the other hand, my mother, Maha, was a natural-born salesperson. She wasn't just good at what she did; she was unstoppable. English wasn't even her first language, but she became one of the top salespeople at companies like Avon and Nutrimetics, consistently ranking at the top and even giving speeches at major conferences. My mum taught me resilience. Her journey, moving to Australia in her 30s and succeeding in a foreign land, showed me what determination and grit looked like in practice. My mother was my biggest cheerleader. I still remember her encouragement when I was in Year 7 and decided to sell coloured keyboard covers to my classmates. It wasn't a huge operation, but it was my first real taste of entrepreneurship. I bought the covers from eBay for about $1.50 each and sold them for $5.

In the end, I made $550, and that moment cemented something important in me. It wasn't just about the money – it was the experience of selling, handling objections, and closing deals. When other students told me they could get the covers cheaper online, I didn't back down. I highlighted the convenience of buying them from me directly. I even pointed out the "higher quality" of my product, though in hindsight, that might have been a bit of a stretch! The lesson was clear: business is about more than just the product; it's about selling the experience, building trust, and understanding human psychology.

My parents, Fayez and Maha, played pivotal roles in shaping my business mindset. My father gave me the structure, discipline, and understanding of operations, while my mother showed me the value of determination, salesmanship, and resilience. They both worked incredibly hard to provide for me and my sister, Kate, ensuring we had a good life in a comfortable, middle-class home. We weren't rich, but we were comfortable. We'd go on a holiday or two each year, but more than that, my parents gave us something far more valuable – a strong work ethic and a belief in our ability to achieve greatness.

As a child growing up in a Christian household, I was also taught the values of respect, service, and faith. These lessons became the bedrock of my personal and professional philosophy. I was always taught to respect my elders and conduct myself with integrity and moral uprightness. These early values stayed with me as I navigated the complexities of business and life. To this day, they inform how I treat others and how I lead my team.

THE BIRTH OF SUCCESS TUTORING

When I was 17, I founded Success Tutoring, but the seeds of that idea were planted long before. My academic journey wasn't an easy one. I was enrolled late in high school and placed in a homeroom that didn't reflect my actual academic level. Initially, I struggled. I was receiving Cs, Ds, and sometimes even Es. I wasn't the kid naturally gifted in academics, but something shifted inside me when I was placed in a "smart class" by accident. Surrounded by high-achieving students, I felt a deep desire to excel. It wasn't just about proving to others that I was capable; it was about proving it to myself.

I worked hard, asked the right questions, and eventually began to see results. By the time I reached Year 11 and 12, I was excelling in subjects like English and Legal Studies. I was even in the top five of my cohort, achieving an ATAR of 93.15. My journey wasn't easy, but it taught me something profound – success in academics and life isn't about where you start; it's about where you're willing to go.

My mother was instrumental during this time, driving me all over Sydney in search of the right maths tutor. Despite attending multiple tutoring centres, I never quite "got" maths. But what I did get was the power of having a mentor – a tutor who believed in me. One tutor in particular, David C, was more than just a tutor; he was a source of inspiration. Before every exam, he would send me messages like, "Good luck, mate. You're going to smash it. I have faith in you!" Those words meant the world to me. They gave me the confidence to keep pushing forwards. David taught me that tutoring wasn't just about the content; it was about connection. It was about having someone in your corner who believed in you.

That experience became the foundation of Success Tutoring's philosophy. At Success Tutoring, we emphasise rapport first, and academics second. I saw firsthand how powerful it was to have someone close in age who could not only teach me but inspire and uplift me. That's what we aim to do at Success Tutoring – we don't just teach; we motivate, inspire, and uplift. We give students the tools they need to believe in themselves.

CHALLENGES AND GROWTH

The early days of Success Tutoring weren't without their challenges. I started the business in my parents' spare room, eventually expanding into the downstairs of their house. There were countless hurdles, from administrative headaches to managing tutors' schedules, but every challenge was an opportunity to learn, grow, and improve. I hired a few friends to help me in the early days, and I quickly realised that building a business was about more than just making money – it was about building relationships, creating systems, and staying focused on the bigger picture.

Looking back, it's clear that the journey wasn't just about tutoring. It was about taking every opportunity to push myself further, demand excellence, and embrace the challenges along the way. I had a vision for Success Tutoring from the start – a vision that extended far beyond those first tutoring sessions in my parents' house. I knew this business would one day be something much bigger, and today, as we've grown into a franchise model, that vision is becoming a reality.

But my story, like yours, is still being written. I want you to understand that success isn't something reserved for a select few. It's something we can all achieve if we're willing to work hard, dream big, and never stop believing in our potential. I didn't come from a wealthy background. I didn't have all the answers. But I had the drive, the passion, and the relentless determination to build something great – and so can you.

PART 1
THE JOURNEY OF SUCCESS TUTORING

CHAPTER 3
HISTORY OF SUCCESS TUTORING

When Success Tutoring began, it was nothing more than a dream, some car magnets, and a spare room in my parents' house. The humble beginnings of what would eventually become a global education system serving thousands of students started with two simple things: a vision and a passion for helping others. While my journey was not without its challenges, every obstacle provided a valuable lesson that ultimately contributed to the growth of Success Tutoring.

EARLY DAYS: PLANTING THE SEEDS

The first steps were small but significant. Initially, I started by tutoring a couple of students in their homes. These were basic, one-on-one sessions. But very quickly, I realised something: I didn't enjoy the process of driving to each student's home. While I loved tutoring, the constant travel was exhausting, and it was clear that something had to change. That's when my dad suggested I tutor in the spare room at home. I took his advice, and little did either of us know that this would be the start of something much bigger than either of us imagined.

I immediately began transforming the spare room into a tutoring space that felt professional and motivational. I printed out a bunch of posters from the internet with inspiring quotes and plastered them on the walls. I tidied up all my study materials and imagined the students who would one day fill the space. At the time, I didn't have any clients, but in my mind, I was already running a successful tutoring business.

Next, I created a Facebook page titled "HSC Success Tutoring", with the initial focus on tutoring students in years 11 and 12. I was 18, had no prior experience running a business, and only had $250 in my bank account, but I used that money to buy two car magnets. I designed them myself, and they were simple, with my phone number, the business name, and a catchy tagline: "Using experience & motivation to achieve results." I slapped them on my parents' car and hoped for the best.

THE FIRST CLIENTS: CRISTIAN AND ANTONIO

But hope alone doesn't get you customers. I posted on social media almost every day for eight months without a single inquiry. It was frustrating and disheartening. I began to wonder if I had made the right decision in pursuing this venture. That's when a friend of my mom's reached out. Her name was Angie, and she connected me to my first two students, Cristian and Antonio, two brothers in high school. I remember the excitement I felt when I first met them. They were my first real clients, and I was determined to give them my best.

I charged their mother $35 per hour for one-on-one sessions. While that might not sound like much, at the time, it felt like I was making a fortune. And more than the money,

I was doing something I loved – helping students improve their academic performance and showing them what they were truly capable of.

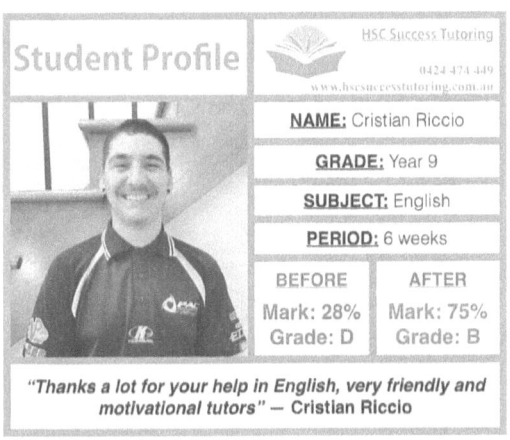

In just four weeks, Cristian and Antonio made remarkable progress. Their grades skyrocketed from Es and Ds to their first A in one subject. It was nothing short of a miracle. That was the moment when I realised this wasn't just about tutoring; this was about changing lives. This was when the spark of something greater ignited in me. I knew this was my path, and I knew that I wanted to take this as far as I could.

THE FIRST TEAM: FRIENDS WHO BECAME TUTORS

As the business began to pick up, I faced another challenge – how to expand. It quickly became apparent that I couldn't do this alone. But hiring people wasn't easy, especially for an 18-year-old with no formal management experience. My first few hires were my friends from school, Ivan B, Thomas T and Thomas D, who were top-performing students. I remember sending Ivan a message on Facebook – yes, we used Facebook for everything back then – about tutoring one of my students before my own sessions.

Here's how that message went: "Hey Champ, great news – first student for you! I tutor this student for English at 11 a.m. every Saturday. Would you be able to tutor him before me at 10 a.m.? Please let me know if your resources will be ready by this week. Also, we'll probably meet beforehand for a small briefing :)"

That was my first "official" message as a manager. We weren't exactly corporate yet, but we were growing. However, as exciting as it was to bring on my friends, it wasn't without its challenges. It was tough balancing friendships with business, and at times, the line became blurred. I found myself trying too hard to be liked by everyone, and as a result, I made compromises that I later regretted.

The truth is, in the first couple of years, I had no real friends. I spent all my time working and trying to build the business. I tried to form bonds with my staff, but sometimes they took advantage of our personal connections. I quickly learned that while friendship is important, boundaries are essential in business. The earlier you set them, the better.

BUILDING SYSTEMS: THE CAT APPROACH
One of the biggest challenges I faced early on was maintaining quality and consistency as we began to grow. After reaching over ten students, I realised that I needed more than just passionate tutors – I needed systems. That's when I developed what I called the "CAT" system: Calendar, Availability, and Timetable.

The CAT system was simple but effective. It was an Excel spreadsheet that allowed tutors to log their schedules, availability, and lesson plans. After each session, tutors were required to record their name, the student they tutored, the date, the subject covered, and the homework assigned. This ensured that every student received consistent attention and guidance, regardless of which tutor they worked with. It was my way of maintaining control over the quality of tutoring even as we expanded to more students and staff.

THE BIG LEAP: FROM HOURLY TUTORING TO MEMBERSHIP
For the first four years, we operated under a traditional hourly model. Students paid per session, and tutors were paid per hour. But as the business grew, this model became unsustainable. We faced several challenges – there was no consistency in revenue, especially during school holidays, and tutors lacked stable working hours.

That's when I made the decision to switch to a gym-style membership model. This was a pivotal moment for the business. Under the new system, students paid a monthly fee, which allowed them flexible scheduling without worrying about re-enrolment each term. Tutors now had consistent hours, and franchise partners enjoyed a steady stream of revenue, even during the slow seasons. It was a win-win for everyone involved.

SCALING UP: THE FIRST COMMERCIAL LEASE

After about 1.5 years of running the business out of my parents' home, it was time to take the next big step – moving into a commercial space. This was a massive leap, both financially and professionally. I had no prior experience with commercial leases, so I did what any young entrepreneur would do – I turned to YouTube for advice.

I also sought help from one of my student's parents, Maria, who was a property conveyancer. She was kind enough to walk me through the basics of negotiating a commercial lease. I'll never forget my first attempt. I approached a landlord and asked for four months' rent-free. His response? "Stop wasting my time." I went back to my car and cried. It was a harsh lesson, but an important one. The real world isn't always kind, and I had to toughen up if I wanted to succeed.

Eventually, I secured a lease for our first official location in Liverpool, NSW, at the age of 20. This was a turning point for Success Tutoring. We were no longer a small, home-based business – we were now a professional operation with a physical presence.

FRANCHISING: THE PATH TO GLOBAL EXPANSION

The decision to franchise Success Tutoring came from a deep-seated desire to take our impact global. I was fortunate to study under Andrew Terry, one of the leading franchise professors in the world, at the University of Sydney. His insights and teachings ignited the spark that led me down the path of franchising.

Our first franchise was sold to one of my ex-teachers. However, no sooner had we celebrated that milestone than COVID-19 hit. The pandemic brought with it a wave of uncertainty, but I remained confident that we could weather the storm. I had always believed that people are the heart of any successful business, and my relationships with both staff and clients became more important than ever during this time.

SUCCESSACADEMY: THE UNIVERSITY OF MICHAEL BLACK

To ensure consistency across all our franchises, I developed the SuccessAcademy, a comprehensive training platform for tutors, managers, and franchise partners. This platform offers industry-leading courses on everything from customer service to sales and marketing. I knew that to maintain our high standards, we had to focus on training, education, and building a strong internal culture.

LOOKING BACK, MOVING FORWARDS

Today, Success Tutoring is set to become one of the world's leading education brands, as we continue to expand into countries such as Australia, New Zealand, the United Kingdom, Singapore, Canada, and the United States. Our vision remains the same: to motivate, inspire, and uplift students. However, our methods have evolved as the business has grown.

I'm incredibly proud of how far we've come, but I'm not surprised. From the very beginning, I envisioned this level of success. I believe that you manifest what you believe you are worthy of, and I always knew that Success Tutoring was destined for greatness.

While the journey has been filled with challenges, it has also been deeply rewarding. We've now tutored over 50,000 students and are on track to reach our goal of 1,000,000 students worldwide. Along the way, I've learned invaluable lessons about business, people, and life itself.

I've been fortunate to be featured on major media platforms like *Forbes*, Channel 7, and Sky News, and in 2024, I was named one of the top 30 franchise executives under 30 in Australia.

But my story isn't over yet. Success Tutoring is only just getting started, and I believe that with the right mindset, work ethic, and passion, there is no limit to what we can achieve.

This is just the beginning.

CHAPTER 4

WHY DO PEOPLE GET TUTORING WRONG?

One of the biggest challenges in education today is the overwhelming amount of misinformation surrounding tutoring. People think they understand it – they believe they know what it is and how it works – but in reality, they often have it completely wrong. They view it as purely academic, a quick fix for poor grades, or a way to stuff more learning into a child's already overburdened schedule. This misconception is pervasive, and it's holding students back from reaching their full potential.

Let's break down some of these common misconceptions. The first is the belief that tutoring is all about learning materials. "The more worksheets, the better!" some might say. But nothing could be further from the truth. When I first started Success Tutoring, I realised that the real value a tutor brings is not in drowning students in homework or practice problems. The true magic happens when a tutor builds rapport, connects with the student, and understands what makes them tick. If a student is motivated – truly inspired to learn – they will go out and find the materials themselves. They will ask questions. They will seek answers. The key is lighting that fire, sparking that passion for learning. Without motivation, all the learning materials in the world won't do a thing.

Another misconception that irks me is the idea that the older or more experienced the tutor, the better they'll be at their job. It's a well-intentioned belief, I understand that, but it's fundamentally flawed. Parents often place too much weight on a tutor's years of experience or qualifications. I've seen many experienced teachers who simply can't relate to students anymore. They've lost that ability to inspire and uplift, and it shows in the student's lack of engagement. Instead of assuming that age or experience equals expertise, we need to look at a tutor's ability to connect, to motivate, to inspire. I'll always hire someone with less experience but more passion and enthusiasm because that's what resonates with students. As the old saying goes, "He who has ears, let him hear." The tutor who listens, understands, and motivates is worth more than a hundred tutors armed with credentials but no heart.

The third misconception that I come across time and time again is the belief that more homework equals better results. Parents will often ask for additional exercises, more problems to solve, more pages to read. But here's the thing: piling on more work doesn't always produce better results. In fact, it often has the opposite effect. Children become overwhelmed, disheartened, and frustrated. What they need isn't more tasks; they need more motivation. When a child is excited about learning, they'll tackle the necessary work themselves – and they'll do it with enthusiasm.

I believe the core of tutoring is simple but often misunderstood: a tutor's job is to motivate, inspire, and uplift.

A great tutor doesn't just teach students *what* to think; they teach students *how* to think. They show them how to find the answers they seek, how to navigate challenges, and how to remain curious. That's where true learning begins. If a student can leave a tutoring session not only with better grades but with a renewed sense of confidence, purpose, and curiosity, then the tutor has done their job.

MOTIVATION IS MORE IMPORTANT THAN LEARNING

It's worth saying that motivation is far more important than learning itself. Without motivation, learning becomes a tedious and painful process, but with it, learning becomes an adventure. A motivated student unlocks untapped potential – they surprise themselves with what they can achieve. This is why at Success Tutoring, our focus is not just on academics. It's about igniting that inner drive. The moment a child is motivated to learn, you've won half the battle.

There's a study that I often refer to, conducted by John Hattie, a renowned education researcher, which states that teachers can have twice the impact on student outcomes as any other factor. But it's not just about teaching content; it's about how the teacher – or tutor – makes the student feel. If a student feels supported, valued, and believed in, they will go further than anyone could have expected. A tutor who motivates is like a gardener who tends to a plant, making sure the environment is perfect for growth. Without that care, the plant may struggle, no matter how fertile the soil or how plentiful the water.

THE MISCONCEPTION OF SELECTIVE SCHOOLING

Another big misunderstanding that parents often have is that tutoring is just for selective schooling. Many parents approach tutoring with the singular goal of getting their child into a selective school, believing that's where success lies. But this is a limiting belief. Tutoring is not just for students aiming for the top 1% or for entrance into elite institutions. It's for everyone.

The demand for tutoring services has skyrocketed across all demographics, and not just because of selective schooling. According to recent studies, nearly one in three students in Australia engage in some form of tutoring. Parents and students alike are beginning to see the value tutoring brings beyond academic results. It's about developing confidence, resilience, and a lifelong love of learning.

Selective schooling may be one path to success, but it's certainly not the only one. A tutor's role is much broader than preparing a child for a selective school exam – it's about helping them navigate their entire educational journey, no matter their destination. A great tutor instils a sense of self-belief, which is a critical skill for life. They help students see beyond grades and exams, fostering personal growth, critical thinking, and problem-solving skills. These are the qualities that will carry them through life, whether or not they end up in a selective school.

THE TUTOR AS A MENTOR, NOT JUST A TEACHER

A tutor is often seen as someone who simply helps students with their homework or explains difficult subjects. But that's a narrow view of what tutoring should be. A great tutor is not just a teacher – they are a mentor. They are someone who can guide the student, not only through academic challenges but through the ups and downs of life as well. A tutor should inspire their students, helping them build a vision for their future and instilling confidence that they can achieve it.

One of the most impactful things a tutor can do is to believe in their student. I've seen students blossom simply because someone took the time to invest in them emotionally, to show them that they are capable of great things. When a student feels supported, their entire outlook changes. Their academic performance improves, but more importantly, their self-esteem skyrockets. They begin to believe in their potential. This, to me, is the true purpose of tutoring.

At Success Tutoring, we often talk about hiring based on personality, not just academic credentials. The reason for this is simple: you can be the smartest person in the world, but if you don't know how to connect with a student, you'll never be an effective tutor. Students don't care how much you know until they know how much you care. Building that trust and rapport is essential. Once the student knows you're on their side, they'll be open to learning. They'll listen to your guidance, and that's when real progress happens.

THE GYM-STYLE MEMBERSHIP MODEL: REVOLUTIONISING TUTORING

One of the biggest innovations we brought to the tutoring industry is our gym-style membership model. In traditional tutoring setups, students would pay by the hour, and it was often inconsistent. If a student missed a session or didn't need help one week, there was a gap in learning, and tutors couldn't maintain a reliable schedule. The gym-style model changed that by offering a membership where students could attend tutoring sessions regularly, just like going to the gym.

This approach had several benefits. It created consistency for students, allowing them to get help whenever they needed it, not just when their parents booked a session. It also made tutoring more affordable, which opened up access to more families. Instead of thinking of tutoring as a luxury, it became a regular part of students' educational routines.

The model also improved retention – students stayed engaged longer because they weren't limited by hourly sessions. And for tutors, it created a steady flow of work, which allowed us to attract and retain the best talent. The gym-style membership model has allowed Success Tutoring to scale in ways traditional tutoring could never have achieved. It's the perfect example of how innovation and thinking outside the box can transform an industry.

WHY THE RAPPORT BUILDING IS THE KEY TO SUCCESS

One of the core principles of Success Tutoring is rapport-building. Tutoring is, at its heart, a relationship-based service. If you think of it as merely transactional – a student pays for help with their studies – you miss out on the transformative power it can have. The relationship between a tutor and student is the foundation for all progress. Without it, no amount of teaching or knowledge will get through.

I remember the first few students I tutored, Cristian and Antonio. It took some time to build rapport with them, to earn their trust. But once that connection was there, their academic progress skyrocketed. In just a few weeks, I saw significant improvements in their performance. It wasn't because I gave them more homework or drilled them with more practice problems. It was because I understood them, I motivated them, and I helped them believe in themselves.

In a world that often emphasises results over relationships, I firmly believe that success in tutoring – and in business – comes from building strong, lasting connections. Whether it's between a tutor and student or a business and its clients, relationships are everything. This is why I challenge the misconception that tutoring is purely academic. It's so much more than that. It's about helping students realise their potential, shaping their mindset, and showing them that they are capable of greatness. Once they believe that, everything else falls into place.

THE RISK OF BUSINESS MISUNDERSTOOD

Another common misconception, especially in the business of tutoring, is that it's inherently risky. Many people view starting a business as a gamble – something only a select few can succeed at. But that's not entirely true, especially within a franchise system like Success Tutoring. A franchise provides a proven model, a roadmap to success. Yes, it still requires hard work, but the risk is significantly reduced because you're not starting from scratch.

People often misunderstand how much effort it takes to replicate the Success Tutoring model. They think it's easy, that all the hard work has already been done. But that's not the case. Franchising, like anything worth doing, requires dedication, focus, and persistence. The SuccessAcademy, our training hub for franchise partners, plays a critical role in correcting these misconceptions. It teaches franchise partners that while the model is proven, the execution still demands hard work, attention to detail, and a commitment to the values of our brand.

Building a business isn't just about following a system; it's about understanding why that system works and being willing to put in the effort to make it successful. Franchising offers a safer path, but it's not without its challenges. However, I truly believe that for those willing to commit, the rewards far outweigh the risks.

TUTORING FOR PERSONAL DEVELOPMENT

To me, tutoring isn't just about improving grades – it's about personal development. It's about shaping a student's character, helping them build resilience, and preparing them for the challenges they'll face in life. When I look back at the students we've helped over the years, it's not just their academic achievements that stand out – it's their growth as individuals. They've become more confident, more capable, and more driven to succeed in all areas of their lives.

Tutoring, when done right, is a tool for unlocking a student's potential. It's not about spoon-feeding them answers or overwhelming them with work. It's about giving them the skills and mindset to succeed on their own. A great tutor empowers students to take ownership of their learning, to be proactive, and to believe in their ability to overcome obstacles.

In many ways, tutoring mirrors the journey of entrepreneurship. Both require persistence, a willingness to learn, and the ability to adapt. Both are about overcoming challenges and finding creative solutions. And both, when successful, lead to personal growth and transformation.

THE MISUNDERSTOOD ROLE OF TUTORS

There's one last misconception I want to address, and that's the misunderstanding of the tutor's role. Tutors are often seen as glorified homework helpers or substitute teachers. But the truth is, they are so much more than that. Tutors are mentors, guides, and motivators. They play a pivotal role in shaping a student's future, not just academically but personally.

A great tutor doesn't judge a student based on their current abilities or grades. They see the potential in every student, and they work tirelessly to bring it out. They believe in their students' dreams and abilities, sometimes even more than the students themselves do. This belief, this unwavering support, is what makes the difference.

That's why at Success Tutoring, we hire based on personality as much as academic results. We look for people who are not just intelligent but who can inspire, uplift, and motivate students. Having good results in school doesn't mean you can teach, and it certainly doesn't mean you can mentor. We look for people who understand that their role as a tutor is to guide students towards becoming the best version of themselves.

TUTORING IS A LIFE-CHANGING TOOL

At its core, tutoring is about so much more than academics. It's about shaping minds, building confidence, and unlocking potential. The misconceptions surrounding tutoring are limiting what it can achieve, but I believe that by addressing these misunderstandings, we can transform the way people view tutoring.

A tutor's role isn't just to teach; it's to inspire, uplift, and motivate. It's to guide students on a journey of personal and academic growth, showing them that they are capable of far more than they ever imagined. When we see tutoring for what it truly is – a tool for unlocking potential – it becomes clear that it's not a luxury but a necessity in today's world.

For those who understand this, the rewards are immense, both for the students and for the tutors. Tutoring, when done right, is a life-changing tool. And that's why I'm so passionate about what we do at Success Tutoring. We're not just improving grades; we're shaping lives. And that, to me, is the greatest success of all.

CHAPTER 5

THE PHILOSOPHY BEHIND SUCCESS TUTORING

When I first launched Success Tutoring, it wasn't just to help students get better grades, and it wasn't even only about teaching. It was something bigger, something deeply rooted in the values and beliefs that had shaped me throughout my life. At its core, Success Tutoring was built to inspire, motivate, and uplift students in a way that goes beyond academics.

In fact, one of the biggest inspirations behind Success Tutoring is rooted in a book that has influenced me profoundly: *The Power of Positive Thinking*. The power of belief, of possibility, and of visualising success has been a guiding light for me, and it is at the heart of Success Tutoring. This isn't just a business; it's a movement driven by the idea that anything is achievable when you put your mind to it.

BUILDING MOTIVATION INTO THE FOUNDATION

When I was younger, I'd spend hours online, searching for motivational quotes. I wanted words that could lift me up when things were tough, and that's exactly what I wanted to give students at Success Tutoring. So, when I started this journey, I went online, found inspiring posters, and framed them on the walls of that very first room we used. In fact, in the very beginning, our slogan was "Using experience & motivation to achieve results." It was simple, but it was the essence of what I wanted Success Tutoring to be.

Those posters still exist, and even now, every Success Tutoring centre is filled with that same positive energy. The colours, the atmosphere, and the motivation are in every corner of our centres. The blue and orange on our signs aren't just colours – they're symbols of confidence, energy, and the unshakeable belief that we have in every student who walks through our doors. The reason why all Success Tutoring centres have vinyl timber flooring is because that represents the timber flooring that was at my parents' house when Success Tutoring started. That is symbolic of the foundations of Success Tutoring. The colours used are bold and stand out, and I love that because they're reminders that Success Tutoring is a different kind of place, one that is centered on possibility and growth.

POINTS, PRIZES, AND THE LESSONS OF REAL-WORLD VALUE

From the start, one of the things I wanted to do was make learning valuable in a way that went beyond just grades. In Success Tutoring, students earn points for their efforts, which they can use for prizes. But it's more than just an incentive system. It's a way for students to understand the power of hard work, persistence, and saving. The points and prizes system teaches students valuable lessons about life, mirroring the way we work with money, effort, and reward. We don't only reward based on results; we reward effort and participation, because sometimes, just showing up and giving your best is what matters most.

I want students to understand that life is about what you put in, not just about what you get out of it. I want them to feel that every point they earn is a reflection of their effort, resilience, and determination. This philosophy is embedded in every Success Tutoring centre, and it's a simple reminder that small steps add up to big accomplishments.

DESIGNING A CURRICULUM FOR TRUE LEARNING

One of the core elements that make Success Tutoring different is the curriculum we've designed. We believe in breaking information down into small, manageable bites – easy for anyone to understand and designed for self-directed learning. When we build a curriculum for a country, we make it fit that country's needs. And we'll continue to learn and adapt from every place we expand to. One day, we'll create the "Universal Success Curriculum" with everything we've learned from our global journey. But for now, we're committed to building customised, country-specific curriculums that cater to the unique needs of students around the world.

The curriculum is simple on purpose. It's easy to understand, with diagnostics and clear steps to follow. And the best part? It's not just about teaching students how to solve problems, but about equipping them with the tools to think critically, work independently, and develop a real love for learning. When I was in school, maths was my weakest subject. I always struggled with it, and I know firsthand the importance of breaking down complex concepts into easy, bite-sized lessons. This is why our curriculum is designed the way it is – because it works.

OPERATIONS AND CONSISTENCY: THE KEY TO GROWTH

I remember learning about standard operating procedures (SOPs) when I was in university. The idea of having an operations manual that could guide anyone in running a business resonated with me so deeply. It was a game-changer. I started by creating simple instructions for the receptionist I hired to help with admin tasks. Over time, this process evolved into the comprehensive Success Tutoring Operations Manual that we use today. It's not just a document – it's a framework that brings consistency, quality, and clarity to every Success Tutoring centre.

Documenting everything from day one allowed us to grow systematically. We have a clear roadmap that helps us deliver a consistent, high-quality experience to students and parents across all our locations. Having this kind of structure is what makes it possible for us to grow on a global scale, without losing sight of what makes Success Tutoring unique.

MOTIVATE, INSPIRE, UPLIFT: THE CORE VALUES OF SUCCESS TUTORING

In every Success Tutoring centre, you'll find these words: *Motivate, Inspire, Uplift*. These aren't just words on a wall – they're a promise to every student who walks through our doors. They're the foundation of everything we do, and they guide us in how we connect with students, parents, and each other.

Our first priority is always to build rapport with students. I've seen firsthand that students thrive when they feel understood, valued, and believed in. I know that when I felt that from my own tutors, it made all the difference in my confidence and my drive to succeed. We're here to be mentors, motivators, and cheerleaders. And when students feel that, the results naturally follow.

THE 3 PILLARS TO SUCCESS: A WIN-WIN-WIN PHILOSOPHY

The success of any business, especially in the franchise world, depends on a delicate balance between three key stakeholders: the franchise partners, the customers, and the franchisor. At Success Tutoring, we believe that true, sustainable success comes from ensuring that all three stakeholders are not just satisfied but thriving. This balance forms the foundation of our 3 Pillars to Success framework.

1. Franchise Partners

Franchise partners are at the heart of Success Tutoring's growth. They are empowered entrepreneurs who bring our brand to life in local communities. To ensure their success, we provide robust training, ongoing support, and a proven business model that minimises risk while maximising potential.

Statistics show that franchises have a higher success rate than independent businesses. According to the International

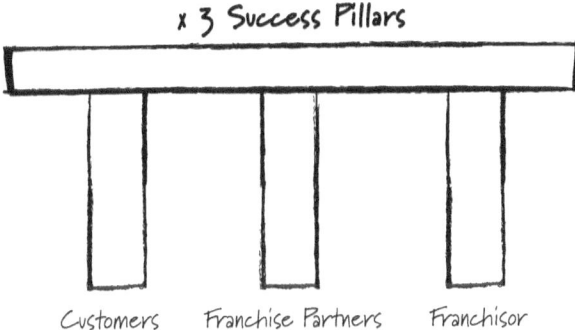

Franchise Association, franchise businesses have a 65% five-year survival rate compared to 20% for independent startups. This success is a direct result of the systems, support, and brand recognition that franchise partners benefit from.

2. Customers

At the core of Success Tutoring's mission is the commitment to motivate, inspire, and uplift students. Happy customers – both students and their families – are the best ambassadors for the brand. We focus on delivering exceptional educational experiences that go beyond academics, fostering personal growth and confidence.

In a recent survey, 93% of parents reported seeing a noticeable improvement in their child's confidence and academic performance after joining Success Tutoring. Happy students lead to long-term loyalty, referrals, and community goodwill, which are invaluable to our franchise partners.

3. Franchisor

The franchisor's role is to build and protect the brand while providing the tools and resources franchise partners need to succeed. At Success Tutoring, we take this responsibility seriously. From developing marketing strategies to continuously improving our training programs, our focus is on creating a strong, scalable system that benefits everyone involved.

The franchisor's success is directly tied to the success of its franchise partners. By focusing on innovation, consistency, and brand reputation, we ensure that the entire network continues to grow and thrive.

WHY THE 3 PILLARS TO SUCCESS MATTER

The 3 Pillars to Success framework creates a win-win-win scenario. When franchise partners feel supported and customers are happy, the franchisor benefits from a growing, reputable brand. This cycle of mutual success is what sets Success Tutoring apart from competitors. It's not just about making money – it's about building a legacy of positive impact.

In the words of Zig Ziglar, "You can have everything in life you want, if you will just help other people get what they want." At Success Tutoring, this philosophy guides everything we do.

A BELIEF IN STUDENTS AND THEIR POTENTIAL

I always tell my team that students have potential beyond what they often realise. When a student feels that someone believes in them, it can be life-changing. At Success Tutoring, we believe in our students, and we're here to help them unlock that potential. Sometimes, the most powerful thing a student can hear is, "I believe in you." That's the core of our tutoring philosophy. We're not here to just impart knowledge; we're here to help students believe in themselves and realise what they're truly capable of.

CHALLENGING THE TRADITIONAL EDUCATION SYSTEM

In many ways, Success Tutoring is a response to the limitations of traditional education. We know that a one-size-fits-all approach doesn't work. The school system often focuses on getting through a standardised curriculum, while we focus on the individual student. Our classes are small, and we customise the experience to fit each student's needs.

Students don't all learn in the same way, and they don't all learn at the same pace. Success Tutoring is designed to offer a learning environment that acknowledges those differences. With a maximum of ten students in a class, we provide more attention, more support, and more personalised guidance. Our structure allows us to meet students where they are and help them grow in the way that works best for them.

GIVING BACK AND CREATING COMMUNITY IMPACT

Community involvement is a huge part of the Success Tutoring philosophy. I'm a big believer in giving back and making a positive impact in the communities we serve. Whether it's through volunteering at local food trucks or creating initiatives that support families and students, I want Success Tutoring to be a force for good in the world. Our centres aren't just places of learning; they're spaces of hope, support, and inspiration.

LOOKING TOWARDS A GLOBAL IMPACT

As we continue to grow, my vision for Success Tutoring expands. We're not just building a tutoring company; we're building a movement that aims to change lives around the world. We'll continue to innovate, adapt, and improve our methods, our curriculum, and our approach. One day, I hope to see Success Tutoring in every corner of the globe, providing access to quality education and motivating, inspiring, and uplifting students everywhere. We'll teach English in countries where it's needed, and we'll expand our reach to make a difference in places that lack access to education.

MICHAEL BLACK

Success Tutoring started as a dream in a spare room, with a few framed quotes and a belief in the power of positive thinking. Today, it's a global network dedicated to helping students reach their full potential. And tomorrow, who knows? The possibilities are limitless. Because at the heart of it all is a simple belief: when we motivate, inspire, and uplift each other, there's nothing we can't achieve.

FROM SOFTWARE ENGINEER TO COMMUNITY LEADER: FINDING PURPOSE WITH SUCCESS TUTORING
Sujit, Success Tutoring Penrith, NSW

For years, I followed the path that society told me would bring success – study hard, get a good degree, and climb the corporate ladder. As a software engineer, I worked for a large IT company, enjoying the stability and security of a well-paying 9-to-5 job. But deep down, I felt stuck. I craved more than just financial security – I wanted purpose, impact, and the chance to make a real difference.

I realised that success isn't just about a stable paycheck. It's about building something meaningful. That's when I discovered Success Tutoring, and I immediately connected with the philosophy behind it: Motivate, Inspire, Uplift. These three words struck a chord with me. I wanted to be part of something bigger – something that didn't just provide academic results but changed lives.

Making the leap from IT engineer to franchise owner was a huge shift, but the transition felt seamless thanks to the SuccessAcademy training and proven systems.

The philosophy of Success Tutoring isn't just a slogan – it's baked into every aspect of the business model. From the way we connect with families to the personalised learning journeys we provide for students, it's all about motivating students to achieve their full potential, inspiring them to believe in themselves, and uplifting them to new heights.

When I launched Success Tutoring Penrith, we started with over 70 foundation members from day one. That initial success wasn't a fluke. It was the result of following a proven process that works. Within just six months, we hit our 120-member milestone, and we haven't looked back since.

The philosophy behind Success Tutoring is what truly sets it apart. It's not just about teaching students – it's about transforming mindsets. The students we work with don't just improve academically – they gain confidence, resilience, and a love for learning. That's what makes this business so fulfilling.

On a personal level, my life has completely transformed. I've gone from sitting behind a desk in a corporate job to being an active member of my community, leading a team, and building a business that makes a difference. The best part? The systems and processes in place at Success Tutoring have given me the freedom to balance my work and family life. I now spend more quality time with my wife and child, something that was hard to manage in my previous job.

One of my proudest moments was being recognised with the national award for 'Most Foundation Members in 2024.' That validation confirmed I made the right decision in joining Success Tutoring.

For anyone sitting on the fence about starting a business, my advice is simple: don't let fear hold you back. Success Tutoring has proven that you're 90% more likely to succeed in a franchise system than going it alone. The systems, support, and community within this network make it possible to achieve things you never thought you could.

I no longer feel stuck. I wake up every day excited to build a legacy, impact my community, and create a future I'm proud of. If you're looking for more than just a career – if you want purpose, impact, and financial freedom – Success Tutoring is the path forwards. It changed my life, and it can change yours too.

CHAPTER 6

BUILDING THE McDONALD'S OF TUTORING

Today, Success Tutoring is set to become one of the world's leading education brands, as we continue to expand into countries such as Australia, New Zealand, United Kingdom, Singapore, Canada and United States.

When people think of McDonald's, they think of consistency, quality, and an experience that feels the same no matter where in the world they are. This is no accident; it is the result of years of perfecting processes, systems, and a franchise model that is now considered the gold standard. It's no surprise that as I envisioned the future of Success Tutoring, the McDonald's model came to mind. Not because of the burgers and fries but because of the global success of their franchise system. When you walk into a McDonald's, you can't tell if it's owned by different people – it feels like one cohesive company. That's exactly what I envision for Success Tutoring.

At Success Tutoring, my goal is to build a tutoring franchise that replicates this consistency. I want every parent and student who walks into one of our centres, whether it's in Sydney, New York, or anywhere else in the world, to experience the same level of service, quality, and success. The same way people go to McDonald's not because of the taste but because they trust the consistency, I want parents to bring their children to Success Tutoring because they know that our centres will motivate, inspire, and uplift their child – no matter where they are.

FRANCHISING: THE KEY TO GLOBAL EXPANSION

Franchising is one of the greatest opportunities to grow a business like Success Tutoring on a global scale. Franchising doesn't just benefit the franchisor; it's a mutually beneficial arrangement where both the franchisor and franchisee stand to gain. Franchise partners can step into a proven business model without the same risk as starting from scratch, and the franchisor can grow the brand without having to provide all the upfront capital. McDonald's has perfected this model, creating a system where their franchise partners become successful entrepreneurs while building up the global brand.

At Success Tutoring, franchising is the key to our long-term vision. By empowering local business owners with the tools, systems, and support they need to replicate our success, we can scale across the globe while maintaining the quality that defines our brand.

SYSTEMS AND PROCESSES: THE FOUNDATION OF CONSISTENCY

One of the greatest lessons I've taken from the McDonald's playbook is the importance of processes and systems. When you build a business designed to scale, you must ensure that everything – from customer service to the product being delivered – is standardised and consistent. At Success Tutoring, we've implemented systems that ensure every centre operates the same way, providing the same high-quality tutoring and motivation that our students need.

I remember staying up late nights with my team, Kate and Caitlin some nights till 11pm building the operations manual. The attention to detail we put into that document was crucial, as it would be the blueprint that every franchise would follow. We knew that for our franchise model to work, everything had to be outlined clearly – from how a centre is set up to how lessons are conducted. This is the level of detail that makes McDonald's successful, and it's the level of detail that will make Success Tutoring the global leader in education.

SUCCESSACADEMY: THE UNIVERSITY OF SUCCESS TUTORING

To maintain the same level of quality across all Success Tutoring franchises, training is paramount. McDonald's has Hamburger University, and we have SuccessAcademy. SuccessAcademy is our world-class training platform where all franchise partners, tutors, and staff learn the Success Tutoring way. Whether it's hiring staff, delivering lessons, or managing day-to-day operations, SuccessAcademy covers it all.

I remember the early days of training when we filmed our first videos with Timothy N on my iPhone. It wasn't perfect, but it got the job done. That's one of the biggest lessons I've learned in business: it doesn't always have to be perfect right away. Over time, we've refined the videos and training programs into what they are today – a polished, professional system that ensures every tutor, franchisee, and employee knows exactly what is expected of them.

BRANDING: MOTIVATE, INSPIRE, UPLIFT

Just like McDonald's, branding is a critical part of Success Tutoring's success. Our branding isn't just about colours or logos – it's about the message and experience we provide. The words "Motivate, Inspire, Uplift" are not just a slogan; they are the foundation of everything we do. We want every student who walks through our doors to leave feeling motivated to achieve their best, inspired to push beyond their limits, and uplifted by the support they receive.

Creating that brand took hours of late-night discussions, brainstorming, and refining. We wanted something that was not only modern but that also captured the heart of what we do. Just like McDonald's golden arches are recognised everywhere, I want the Success Tutoring brand to be synonymous with quality education and student success.

RAPID EXPANSION: SCALING SUCCESS TUTORING GLOBALLY

One of McDonald's key strategies was rapid expansion, and at Success Tutoring, we have the same goal. As we continue to expand, maintaining the quality of our service is paramount. We've designed Success Tutoring to be scalable from day one. That means every process, every system, and every aspect of the business has been created with the intention of replicating it across multiple locations without losing the essence of what makes us unique.

One of the biggest challenges in scaling a business is maintaining quality. As we open more centres across the world, it's important to ensure that each one offers the same experience. That's why we've invested so much time in developing our training systems and processes, ensuring that every tutor and every franchisee is aligned with our mission.

INNOVATION AND ADAPTABILITY: STAYING RELEVANT

Like McDonald's, which constantly introduces new items to its menu while maintaining its core offerings, Success Tutoring must innovate to stay relevant. We are constantly updating our curriculum and learning materials to keep up with the latest educational trends, ensuring that our students receive the best possible education. But while we innovate, we also stay true to our core values: motivating, inspiring, and uplifting students.

Technology plays a huge role in how we scale and innovate. Our Success Tutoring app allows parents to book sessions, track progress, and manage their child's membership seamlessly. This integration of technology makes it easier for us to scale while maintaining a high level of customer service.

CREATING A CULTURE OF SUCCESS

One of the most important lessons I've learned from McDonald's is the importance of creating a strong company culture. At Success Tutoring, we've built a culture of excellence, where everyone – tutors, staff, and franchise partners – is aligned with our mission. We've created a company culture that values hard work, but also innovation, creativity, and a dedication to making a positive impact on our students' lives.

At the core of that culture is the belief that every student has the potential to succeed. We don't just focus on academic results; we focus on helping students build confidence, resilience, and a love for learning. This culture is something we foster in every centre, and it's what sets us apart from other tutoring services.

BUILDING THE LEGACY: THE McDONALD'S OF TUTORING

Ultimately, the goal of building the McDonald's of tutoring is about more than just financial success. It's about creating a global brand that changes lives. McDonald's revolutionised the fast-food industry, and I want Success Tutoring to revolutionise education. I want Success Tutoring to be a brand that is known around the world for providing students with the tools they need to succeed, not just in school but in life.

Building the McDonald's of tutoring means creating a business that is scalable, consistent, and impactful. It's about offering franchise partners the opportunity to build their own successful businesses while maintaining the high standards that define Success Tutoring. It's about providing parents and students with a tutoring service they can trust, no matter where they are in the world.

As we continue to grow and expand, I remain focused on the bigger picture: helping over 1,000,000 students across the globe achieve their full potential. Just like McDonald's has left a lasting legacy in the fast-food industry, I want Success Tutoring to leave a lasting legacy in the world of education.

CHAPTER 7

THE SUCCESSACADEMY (UNIVERSITY OF MICHAEL BLACK)

When I first started Success Tutoring, I quickly realised that scaling the brand would require more than just passion and hard work – it would require the right systems and training to maintain consistency across every location. That's when the idea for SuccessAcademy was born. I wanted to create a platform that not only trained people correctly but also shared the lessons I had learned through trial and error, helping others avoid the mistakes I made along the way.

You see, one of the biggest values for any incoming franchise partner is that they don't have to reinvent the wheel. They don't have to waste time and money figuring out what works and what doesn't. With the SuccessAcademy, we've streamlined the training process to focus on what actually drives success, ensuring that every franchisee can become profitable quickly by sticking to what we know works.

THE BIRTH OF THE "UNIVERSITY OF MICHAEL BLACK"

Why call it the University of Michael Black? Because the essence of Success Tutoring was built around my personal values and experiences, particularly from my own time in high school. I believe deeply in motivating, inspiring, and uplifting students to reach their full potential, and these core principles shaped the foundation of our business. The SuccessAcademy embodies this same philosophy – it's a holistic training program designed to teach franchise partners not just how to run a tutoring business, but how to live and breathe the mission of Success Tutoring.

The academy is structured like a university because the training goes beyond basic operational tasks. It's about leadership, mindset, and building a business from the ground up. Just like in any good university, we provide the tools and knowledge, but it's up to the individuals to take those lessons and apply them to their own journey.

THE MISSION BEHIND SUCCESSACADEMY

The mission of SuccessAcademy is straightforward: to provide the best training and development program for every tutor, manager, assistant manager, and franchise partner within the Success Tutoring network. We're not just building businesses; we're building leaders. To create the most successful franchise system in the world, we need to have the best training in the world – and that's what SuccessAcademy delivers.

Traditional educational systems often fail because they focus on outdated, face-to-face training methods that vary in quality. SuccessAcademy, on the other hand, provides a scalable, uniform solution. The platform ensures that every single franchisee and employee receives the same high-quality training, no matter where they're located.

THE TUTOR'S CREED

One important aspect of SuccessAcademy, is The Tutor's Creed – which is a transformative philosophy that revolutionises the very essence of what it means to be a tutor. It is not just a set of principles – it is a movement, a mission to redefine education as we know it. This creed elevates the role of a tutor far beyond the confines of academics. Tutors are not merely transmitters of knowledge; they are life-changers, dream-enablers, and purpose-igniters. They shape futures, mold mindsets, and inspire greatness in every student they touch.

CORE PRINCIPLES OF THE TUTOR'S CREED

1. **Motivate**
   "A motivated student is an unstoppable learner."
   A tutor's first role is to ignite a spark in their student. Motivation drives curiosity, resilience, and the desire to learn, often more than academic material alone.

Tutors must understand their students' goals, fears, and unique challenges to fuel their inner drive.
Actions:
- Celebrate small wins to build confidence.
- Use stories, examples, and real-world connections to make learning exciting.
- Help students see the long-term value of their efforts.

2. **Inspire**

"Inspiration plants the seeds of greatness."

Tutors are role models. By sharing their own stories, lessons, and struggles, they show students what's possible. Inspiration is about helping students believe in their abilities and dream bigger than they ever thought possible.
Actions:
- Lead by example with passion and integrity.
- Share stories of overcoming challenges, especially in academics or life.
- Expose students to the possibilities beyond their current circumstances.

3. **Uplift**

"Encouragement is the foundation of transformation."

A tutor should create a safe, supportive environment where students feel valued and understood. When students feel uplifted, they are more likely to persevere through challenges and grow into confident learners.
Actions:
- Build trust by genuinely listening to students' concerns.
- Offer constructive feedback that builds self-esteem rather than tearing it down.
- Be their cheerleader, reminding them of their potential even when they doubt themselves.

4. **Teach How to Think, Not What to Think**
   "Education is not about answers; it's about questions."
   A great tutor fosters critical thinking and problem-solving skills rather than rote memorisation. They empower students to become independent thinkers who can approach challenges creatively and confidently.
   Actions:
   - Encourage curiosity by asking open-ended questions.
   - Teach students how to find information rather than giving them all the answers.
   - Promote a growth mindset by showing them how mistakes are opportunities to learn.

5. **Build Rapport Before Academics**
   "Connection precedes correction."
   A tutor must establish a strong relationship with their student. When students feel understood and respected, they are more open to learning and willing to engage in the process.
   Actions:
   - Take time to understand the student's personality, interests, and challenges.
   - Use humour, empathy, and authenticity to break down barriers.
   - Make the learning environment comfortable and relatable.

6. **Empower the Student Beyond Academics**
   "Tutoring isn't just about grades; it's about growth."
   The role of a tutor extends beyond academics. A tutor can guide students in building life skills such as time management, goal setting, resilience, and self-confidence.
   Actions:
   - Help students set personal goals and track their progress.

- Teach them how to manage their time and prioritise tasks effectively.
- Offer mentorship and advice for life outside the classroom.

THE TUTOR'S CREED IN PRACTICE

The Tutor's Creed isn't just an idea – it's a set of actionable commitments that every tutor should embody. Here's how it could look in practice:

The Tutor's Creed:
1. I commit to motivating my students to believe in their potential.
2. I commit to inspiring my students through my actions and stories.
3. I commit to uplifting my students by creating a positive and supportive environment.
4. I commit to teaching my students how to think critically and solve problems independently.
5. I commit to building rapport and trust before diving into academics.
6. I commit to empowering my students to succeed not just in school, but in life.

The Tutor's Creed can transform how tutoring is perceived and delivered, creating a legacy of motivated, inspired, and uplifted students.

REAL-LIFE STORIES BEHIND THE TRAINING

One of the core aspects of the SuccessAcademy is the fact that it's based on real-life experiences – my experiences. For instance, when we first designed the layout for our centres, I bootstrapped the business and personally installed the flooring at our Liverpool location. I imported the materials from China and, in theory, it was a DIY job that anyone could do. But after spending an entire day trying to lay the flooring, exhausted and frustrated, I learned an important lesson: sometimes it's better to pay a professional and focus on what you do best.

That experience is embedded in the SuccessAcademy. It's not just about saving money or doing everything yourself – it's about learning when to delegate and knowing your strengths. These are lessons I want every franchise partner to understand because they're key to running a successful business.

Another story I share in the academy is about my early days of hiring staff. I remember being just as nervous as the people I was interviewing, meeting them in local cafes like Blue Star Café in Stockland. It was an informal process, and I quickly realised that hiring isn't something you should take lightly. That's why SuccessAcademy has dedicated modules on hiring the right people and how to conduct professional interviews – because your team is the foundation of your business.

THE INFLUENCE OF MENTORSHIP AND EXPERIENCE

When I decided to franchise Success Tutoring, I sought out advice from some of the best in the industry. One of my most valuable mentors was Doug Downer, a franchise consultant with a wealth of experience working with brands like McDonald's. Doug helped me understand the importance of creating strong operational procedures, and his guidance was instrumental in the creation of SuccessAcademy.

I'll never forget my first meeting with Doug at his office in Chippendale, Sydney. His office felt like a man cave, complete with arcade games and a massage chair, but what impressed me the most was his genuine belief in what I was building. He gave me a signed copy of his book and wrote, "Michael, congratulations on what you have achieved at such a young age. Your business is ready to skyrocket."

Doug's advice helped me refine our systems and procedures, and it inspired me to create a training program that would set franchise partners up for success from day one. SuccessAcademy is filled with lessons like these – lessons learned from both triumphs and challenges.

EMPOWERING FRANCHISE PARTNERS AND STAFF

One of the greatest benefits of SuccessAcademy is the empowerment it gives to our franchise partners and staff. Many of our franchise partners come into the business without any prior experience running a company, and that's okay. SuccessAcademy provides them with everything they need to succeed, from how to manage day-to-day operations to how to lead a team effectively.

We've seen incredible results: 90% of tutors report increased confidence in their teaching abilities after completing the foundational modules, and 85% of tutors who went through our advanced leadership training were promoted to managerial roles within 18 months. These aren't just numbers – they're real people whose lives and careers have been transformed through training.

LEARNING FROM MISTAKES

I've always believed that you learn more from your mistakes than your successes, and that's a key principle of SuccessAcademy. One of the most challenging moments in my journey was when I had to fire a tutor who had been with us for a while. I received a call from a parent saying that this tutor had asked them if they wanted to continue their tutoring sessions outside of the Success Tutoring centre – essentially trying to steal the customer.

I confronted the tutor after his shift and asked him straight up if the accusation was true. He admitted it, and I had to let him go. It was a difficult decision, but it taught me a valuable lesson about integrity and loyalty. That's why we've built clear guidelines into SuccessAcademy, outlining what is and isn't acceptable when it comes to our business.

CONSTANT IMPROVEMENT AND FUTURE GROWTH

SuccessAcademy isn't a static platform. We're constantly improving and updating the content based on feedback from our franchise partners and the latest trends in education and business. This commitment to continuous improvement ensures that we stay ahead of the curve and that every person in the organisation has the most up-to-date training.

Looking ahead, I see SuccessAcademy evolving beyond just training for Success Tutoring. My long-term vision is for it to become a platform for personal and business development, helping people in all industries unlock their full potential. It's more than just a training program – it's the foundation of the University of Michael Black, a place where people are taught by those who have actually walked the path, not just by those who have studied theory.

THE ACADEMY

If there's one message I want readers to take away from this chapter, it's that SuccessAcademy is the key to unlocking your potential. Whether you're a tutor, a manager, or a franchise partner, the training you receive through this platform will set you up for success in both your personal and professional life.

You don't have to figure it all out on your own. SuccessAcademy has been built on the lessons I've learned, the mistakes I've made, and the victories I've celebrated. It's a roadmap to success, and I believe that with the right mindset, anyone can achieve greatness.

So, as you move forwards in your journey, remember this: success isn't just about what you know – it's about how you apply it. SuccessAcademy is here to guide you every step of the way, and I'm excited to see where it will take you.

FROM CLASSROOM TO BUSINESS: A TEACHER'S JOURNEY TO MAKING A BIGGER IMPACT

Laurise, Success Tutoring Harris Park, NSW

After more than 20 years as a primary school teacher, I thought I had seen it all – the highs and lows of education, the joy of seeing students succeed, and the challenges that come with helping children unlock their potential. But as much as I loved teaching, there was always a part of me that felt I could do more. I wanted to create something that went beyond the traditional classroom. I wanted to build a space where children could not only improve academically but also grow in confidence and resilience.

That's when I discovered Success Tutoring.

Becoming a franchise owner was a big leap for me. I had spent my entire career in schools, following structured systems and routines. The idea of running my own business was both exciting and intimidating. But with the guidance and support of the SuccessAcademy and the proven processes of Success Tutoring, I quickly realised that this was my chance to combine my passion for education with a new challenge – entrepreneurship.

The training provided by SuccessAcademy was invaluable. It wasn't just about understanding the business model; it was about mastering the systems, processes, and mindset needed to succeed as a franchise owner. The Success Tutoring model is designed for scalability, and every step of the process – from marketing to student engagement – was laid out clearly. The comprehensive support gave me the confidence to launch my centre successfully and avoid the pitfalls that many first-time business owners face.

Launching Success Tutoring Harris Park was one of the most rewarding experiences of my life. From day one, we had over 70 students enrolled, a testament to the need for a supportive, motivating learning environment in our community. Our rapid success even caught the attention of *The Sydney Morning Herald*, one of Australia's largest newspapers. Being featured in such a prominent publication was a proud moment that validated my decision to take this leap.

What sets Success Tutoring apart is its focus on motivating, inspiring, and uplifting students – principles that I've carried with me throughout my teaching career. Now, as a business owner, I'm able to make a bigger impact. I have the flexibility to shape the learning environment in a way that best supports each child's unique needs. I've built a team of dedicated tutors who share my passion for helping students thrive. And I've seen firsthand how our approach transforms students – not just academically, but emotionally and socially as well.

Running my own tutoring centre has given me freedom I never thought possible. I'm no longer bound by the limitations of the traditional school system. I have the opportunity to mentor not only students but also my team, ensuring that we create a lasting impact in the lives of everyone who walks through our doors.

For teachers considering a career change, my advice is simple: take the leap. The SuccessAcademy gives you the tools, processes, and ongoing support to make the transition from educator to entrepreneur seamless. If you've ever thought, *"I want to make a bigger difference,"* franchising with Success Tutoring is the perfect way to do it. It's not just about running a business – it's about building a legacy. And for me, that legacy is one of empowerment, growth, and endless possibilities.

PART 2

MINDSET & EXECUTION

CHAPTER 8

IDEAS ARE WORTHLESS WITHOUT EXECUTION

In business and in life, ideas are plentiful. We all have them – bright sparks of inspiration that hit us in the shower, while driving, or just before bed. We often find ourselves thinking, "This could change everything." But here's the hard truth: an idea alone is worthless if it's not followed by execution. Execution is everything – it's what separates dreamers from achievers, talkers from doers. Without taking action, ideas are just fantasies, daydreams floating around without any chance of becoming a reality.

WHAT IS EXECUTION?

Execution is the bridge between an idea and its reality. It's not just a matter of doing – it's about doing the right things at the right time, with the right people. Execution involves process, strategy, timing, and a certain amount of gut feeling. It's trial and error, adaptation, and resilience. In short, it's about turning an idea into something tangible. Ideas are commonplace, but those who execute well are rare.

Take, for example, Facebook and MySpace. Before Facebook existed, MySpace was king. But MySpace lacked execution in the long term – it didn't adapt, innovate, or improve its user experience fast enough. Facebook, on the other hand, executed their vision brilliantly, learning from MySpace's mistakes, growing faster, and adapting to user needs. The result? Facebook became one of the greatest companies in the world. It wasn't just the idea of a social network that made Facebook what it is today – it was the ability to execute.

This same principle applies to tutoring. Anyone can come up with the idea of a new educational program, but very few know how to execute it effectively. It's not just about creating a curriculum; it's about marketing it to the right audience, building partnerships with businesses, hiring the right tutors, and ensuring that everything – from pricing to student engagement – runs smoothly.

EXECUTION VS IDEAS

One of the most important distinctions in business is the difference between generating ideas and executing them. Ideas can be fleeting – they come and go – but execution is what brings them to life. I've often been asked, "Why don't you make people sign NDAs (Non-Disclosure Agreements) before discussing your franchise model? Aren't you worried they'll steal your idea?" But the truth is, I'm not. In the modern business world, ideas aren't secrets to be guarded – they're open-source. What matters is not who has the idea but who can execute it better.

Think of Coca-Cola. The recipe is famously secret, but let's be honest – if someone stole the recipe today, would it really matter? Would that person be able to replicate the decades of execution that have built Coca-Cola into a global powerhouse? The same goes for tutoring businesses. People can copy your worksheets, your lesson plans, or your pricing models, but they can't steal your ability to execute better than they do. It's your personality, your relationships with students and parents, and your commitment to motivating, inspiring, and uplifting that make you successful. Execution is where the real power lies.

Many people think they need to hold their ideas close and protect them, fearing that someone will steal them. But here's the reality: execution is the only thing that can't be stolen. You can share your ideas openly, but what matters is how well you bring those ideas to life. If someone takes your idea but can't execute it, it remains nothing but a fleeting thought.

EXECUTION DNA

In the world of business, ideas are abundant, but execution is what separates the successful from the stagnant. At Success Tutoring, we believe that execution isn't just a skill – it's part of your DNA. I call it *Execution DNA*, and understanding it is essential to becoming a successful entrepreneur. You must have the DNA *for* success.

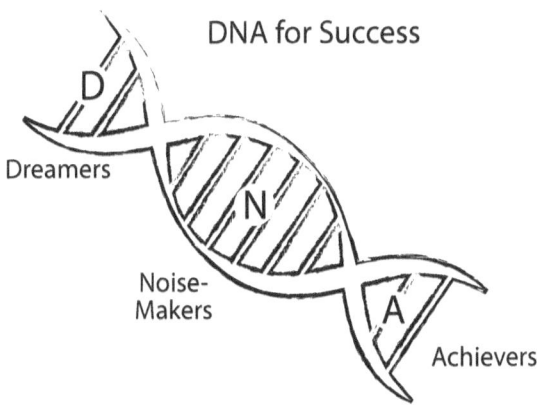

Execution DNA breaks down into three distinct types of people:

D – DREAMERS

Dreamers are the thinkers, the idea generators. They excel at envisioning possibilities and crafting detailed plans. Their minds are filled with creative solutions and innovative ideas. However, there's a critical flaw: they rarely take action.

Dreamers often get stuck in their heads, lost in the planning phase without ever moving forwards. They talk about what *could* be but fail to make it a reality.

Key Trait: Vision without action.
Outcome: Unfulfilled potential.

N – NOISE-MAKERS

Noise-Makers are the opposite of Dreamers. They act quickly and often without much thought or strategy. To the outside world, they appear busy, always in motion. But there's a problem: their actions lack direction.

Noise-Makers prioritise activity over achievement. They make noise, but it rarely results in meaningful progress. Mistakes are frequent because they focus on doing rather than thinking.

Key Trait: Action without strategy.
Outcome: Effort without meaningful progress.

A – ACHIEVERS

Achievers strike the perfect balance between thinking and doing. They have the vision of Dreamers and the action-oriented mindset of Noise-Makers, but with one key difference: they adapt and learn along the way.

Achievers understand that execution isn't a one-and-done process. It requires continuous improvement, resilience, and adaptability. They think before they act, but they don't get stuck in analysis paralysis. They act with purpose and adjust their course as needed.

Key Trait: Vision combined with execution.
Outcome: Meaningful, lasting results.

SUMMARY OF DNA TYPES

- **D – Dreamers:** Think, overthink, but rarely do.
- **N – Noise-Makers:** Do without thinking, making mistakes along the way.
- **A – Achievers:** Think, act, and adapt to achieve success.

Understanding your Execution DNA type is the first step in improving your approach to execution. The goal is to move towards becoming an Achiever – a person who balances vision with action and adapts as they go.

WHY EXECUTION DNA MATTERS

Execution DNA is more than just a framework – it's a mindset shift. By identifying where you fall on the spectrum of Dreamers, Noise-Makers, and Achievers, you can take steps to improve your execution skills.

Many people think success is reserved for those with the best ideas. But in reality, success belongs to those who can take those ideas and bring them to life. Achievers are the ones who understand that execution isn't about perfection – it's about progress. They take calculated risks, learn from their mistakes, and keep moving forwards.

At Success Tutoring, we focus on cultivating Achievers. Our systems and processes are designed to help franchise partners move from being Dreamers or Noise-Makers to becoming true Achievers. Execution isn't just something you do; it's part of who you are. It's in your DNA.

HOW TO DEVELOP YOUR EXECUTION DNA

To become an Achiever, start by recognising your tendencies. Are you more of a Dreamer, stuck in planning mode? Or are you a Noise-Maker, acting without a clear strategy? Once you know where you stand, take intentional steps to change your behaviour:

1. **If you're a Dreamer:** Set deadlines for action. Don't wait for the perfect moment to start.
2. **If you're a Noise-Maker:** Pause to think before you act. Develop a strategy before diving in.
3. **If you're an Achiever:** Keep refining your process. Stay adaptable and resilient.

Execution DNA is about becoming the kind of entrepreneur who gets things done. It's about turning vision into reality and achieving meaningful, lasting results.

THE PATH TO ACHIEVING SUCCESS

At the heart of Execution DNA is a simple truth: execution is what drives success. You can have all the ideas in the world, but without the ability to execute, they remain just ideas. By developing your Execution DNA, you position yourself to be a leader who doesn't just dream or make noise – you achieve.

The choice is yours: will you remain a Dreamer or Noise-Maker? Or will you become an Achiever and build something truly impactful?

GENERATING IDEAS AND BRIDGING THE GAP

Let's talk about generating ideas. Ideas are everywhere, and they often come at unexpected moments. For me, it's in the shower or just before bed. The important thing is to capture them. Keep a notebook by your side or use an app to jot them down. But remember this: ideas are just the first step. Execution is the gap between inspiration and success, and it's a gap that not everyone knows how to bridge.

So how do you bridge that gap? It starts with confidence. Confidence in your ability to take action is essential. You need to be decisive, even if you don't always make the right decision the first time. Quick decisions, followed by quick course corrections, are far better than hesitating until the opportunity passes. You learn through action, not inaction.

A great example of this is when we transitioned Success Tutoring from a traditional hourly model to a gym-style membership model. The idea was simple enough, but executing it was a monumental task. We knew the traditional model wasn't working, especially during COVID. I sat in my parents' backyard and sketched out what the "perfect" tutoring model would look like – a single pricing structure, group tutoring, easy-to-manage bookings through an app.

But even with a solid idea, execution was tough. Our first franchise partner hated the idea. It was a hard pill to swallow. I knew this model was the key to Success Tutoring's future, but convincing others to see that vision was challenging. Yet, I persisted. We spent months testing, refining, and finally implementing the model. It wasn't the idea that saved us – it was the persistence and execution behind it.

THE ROLE OF THE RIGHT TEAM

No one can execute perfectly on their own. Having the right team in place is critical to successful execution. A good team brings ideas to life, but a great team helps you navigate the challenges that come with it. The qualities I look for in my team are passion, resilience, and the ability to make quick, confident decisions.

"First who, then what," as Jim Collins said in his book *Good to Great*. This means that building the right team is the most important step before deciding on what you will do or how you will do it. With the right people, even the most difficult execution becomes possible.

When you're building a business, especially in something as personal and trust-based as tutoring, you need people who can execute with the same passion and care as you do. It's not just about filling roles – it's about making sure the people you bring on board align with your vision and are as committed to execution as you are.

TO EXECUTE WELL, YOU MUST EXECUTE ON THE RIGHT THINGS

Ever wondered why some people run extremely successful businesses which become global empires and others are stuck in the day-to-day operations of the business? I've seen people who have run a bread shop for over 35 years, yet the business never grows. They're caught in a cycle of maintaining the business rather than growing it.

The difference between these people and YOU is that you need to focus on income-generating activities. As a business owner, you can focus on two categories of tasks: Maintenance Mode and Growth Mode.

MILLIONAIRE TUTOR

Maintenance Mode (Delegate These)	Growth Mode (Do These)
These are the day-to-day operational tasks that keep your business running but don't necessarily grow it. Tasks like: • Managing day-to-day scheduling for tutors and students. • Handling basic inquiries and customer service issues. • Processing invoices, payments, and payroll. • Updating student and parent records. • Monitoring student progress reports and tutor feedback. • Organising routine parent-tutor meetings. • Maintaining the cleanliness and appearance of the tutoring centre. • Managing supplies and equipment repairs. These tasks are essential, but they don't generate new revenue. You need to delegate them to someone else so that you can focus on Growth Mode.	These are the tasks that directly contribute to growing your business and generating more income. Tasks like: • Running targeted paid ad campaigns to attract new leads. • Creating partnerships with local schools and organisations for referrals. • Hosting community events or workshops to showcase the tutoring centre. • Offering free trial sessions to potential members. • Conducting personalised consultations with parents to address their concerns. • Developing a lead nurturing system using automated email sequences. • Designing and executing a strategic marketing plan that targets specific demographics. • Launching referral programs to encourage existing members to bring in friends or family. You need to be absolutely FOCUSED 100% on Growth Mode tasks 90% of the time (if not more). These are the activities that will take your business to the next level. Growth Mode tasks create momentum, build brand awareness, and drive revenue. If you're stuck doing maintenance tasks all day, your business will remain stuck too.

OVERCOMING CHALLENGES IN EXECUTION

Execution isn't easy. One of the greatest challenges I faced was transitioning our business model during a global pandemic. I had just sold two franchises, but neither was performing well. I knew that if we didn't make a change, the company might collapse. The idea of the gym-style model came to me in a moment of clarity, but getting it off the ground wasn't smooth sailing. When our first franchise partner rejected it, I felt defeated.

But here's the thing about execution – it's not about doing everything perfectly the first time. It's about staying resilient, pushing forwards, and being confident in your vision even when others don't see it yet. I had to pivot, adapt, and find new ways to communicate the value of our model. Eventually, the shift paid off, but it took resilience and a firm belief in our ability to execute.

STAYING FOCUSED ON EXECUTION

In a world full of distractions, maintaining focus on execution can be challenging. There will always be setbacks, obstacles, and reasons to delay action. The key is to stay focused on your end goal and break down the path to success into smaller, manageable steps.

One of the personal strategies I've found most effective is creating a vision board. Seeing your goals visually laid out helps keep you focused on what really matters. Along with that, creating small, daily tasks that contribute to your larger goals ensures that you're making progress every day. Execution isn't about one giant leap – it's about consistent, deliberate action.

Another important element of staying focused is maintaining accountability. Whether it's checking in with your team or holding yourself to deadlines, having a system of accountability keeps execution on track. Without accountability, it's easy to let things slip through the cracks or allow procrastination to creep in.

RESILIENCE IS KEY

Resilience is at the heart of good execution. There will always be obstacles along the way, but how you respond to setbacks is what defines your success. Execution requires resilience, the ability to pivot when necessary, and the willingness to push forwards even when things get tough.

When we transitioned Success Tutoring to our membership model, we lost some staff members who didn't believe in the new direction. We faced resistance from some parts of the team, and it wasn't easy. But resilience helped us push through. We believed in the vision, and we knew that in order to succeed, we had to stick to our execution plan.

LESSONS LEARNED AND SUCCESS STORIES

We've made plenty of mistakes along the way. But what's important is that we learn from them. Execution is never perfect, but each mistake offers an opportunity to improve. One of the biggest lessons I've learned is the importance of communication. Often, I assumed that everyone on the team understood the direction we were heading in, only to find out later that there was confusion. Clear, consistent communication is essential to successful execution.

One of our greatest success stories was the launch of our gym-style membership model. It was a risky move, and there were moments when I doubted whether it would work. But by staying focused, adapting when necessary, and executing relentlessly, we made it a reality. It wasn't the idea alone that made it work – it was the daily execution that brought it to life.

MOTIVATING OTHERS TO TAKE ACTION

One of the most powerful ways to motivate others is to help them see the end goal clearly. Clarity of vision is the driving force behind action. When people understand what they're working towards and why, they're more likely to take action. Set clear, actionable goals, and break them down into small, achievable steps.

Motivation comes from seeing progress. When you can break a large goal down into smaller steps and see each one being completed, it builds momentum. Celebrate small wins along the way, because each small victory brings you closer to the big picture.

Another powerful motivator is reminding yourself, and those around you, of the impact their actions will have. Why does this matter? What will happen once you execute this idea? The more clearly you can connect the action to a meaningful result, the more driven people will be to see it through.

EXECUTION CHANGES THE LANDSCAPE OF TUTORING

The future of education is dynamic, and execution will be what defines the next generation of successful tutoring businesses. The landscape of tutoring and education is constantly evolving, and we need to stay flexible and adaptable in our approach. The ability to execute consistently – no matter the obstacles – will determine who rises to the top.

At Success Tutoring, we've created a culture that values execution. We don't waste time on unnecessary meetings or endless discussions. We prioritise getting things done. As the company grows, this culture of execution will be critical to maintaining our success and staying ahead of the curve.

In the tutoring world, we often see competitors come and go, but what sets apart those who last is their ability to execute. Tutoring businesses aren't just about providing educational materials or offering one-off lessons. It's about creating long-term systems that deliver real results for students, parents, and the business. Without effective execution, even the most promising tutoring business will fall behind.

START EXECUTING NOW

To all aspiring entrepreneurs and franchise partners: stop waiting for the perfect moment to execute. There is no perfect moment. The time to start is now. Make decisions quickly, learn from your mistakes, and keep moving forwards. Don't get caught up in the trap of overthinking. Ideas are worthless without action.

Here are a few actionable steps to help you execute better:

1. **Set clear, actionable goals** and break them down into smaller steps.
2. **Develop a routine for decision-making** – learn to make quick decisions and adjust along the way.
3. **Build a team that shares your vision** and is as committed to execution as you are.
4. **Learn from mistakes quickly** and use them as stepping stones to success.
5. **Stay focused on the bigger picture** – always remember why you started.
6. **Create accountability systems** – check in with your team or yourself to ensure progress is being made daily.
7. **Stay resilient** – understand that execution is never smooth, but persistence through challenges will pay off.

If you're reading this as an aspiring franchise partner or business owner, the most important thing you can do is start taking action today. Don't wait for the stars to align, don't wait for the perfect circumstances, and don't be afraid to make mistakes along the way. Each step you take gets you closer to your goal, even if the path isn't perfectly straight.

Remember, you're one execution away from success. Every great business, every innovation, and every achievement was born not just from an idea but from the persistence and grit it took to make that idea a reality.

THE CULTURE OF EXECUTION

At Success Tutoring, we built a culture of execution. We don't believe in overthinking or stalling for perfection. The focus is always on getting things done efficiently and effectively. A good business doesn't just have great ideas – it has great people who know how to turn those ideas into action.

Creating a culture of execution in your business means:
- **Empowering your team** to make decisions and act quickly.
- **Rewarding execution** rather than just ideas.
- **Focusing on results**, not just tasks.

One of the ways we foster execution at Success Tutoring is by removing the red tape. Long emails, countless meetings, and drawn-out approval processes are enemies of execution. We prioritise action, and we make it clear that as long as you're moving forwards, mistakes can be fixed, and decisions can be refined. But if you don't execute, you're stuck in place.

Execution is a skill that every team member must develop. It's not just for the CEO or the managers – it's for everyone. Everyone in the company should be a doer.

In the end, the difference between success and failure comes down to execution. You can have all the brilliant ideas in the world, but if you can't turn those ideas into action, they remain nothing more than wishful thinking. Execution requires courage, confidence, and a relentless focus on the end goal.

As the famous saying goes, "Vision without execution is just hallucination." It's time to stop dreaming and start doing.

Make today the day you begin executing on your ideas, and you'll be amazed at what you can achieve.

Success is not just for the people with the best ideas – it's for the ones who have the determination to see their ideas through to the end. So, what are you waiting for? Start executing today and turn your ideas into the reality they were meant to be.

CHAPTER 9

POLITICS IS CANCER

In every organisation, there are invisible threats that, if left unchecked, can quietly eat away at its foundation, just like cancer. Politics is one of those threats. It spreads silently, often unnoticed until it has already done damage. Internal politics – when people are more focused on personal gain than the success of the organisation – has the potential to bring down even the most promising businesses. And once it takes hold, it spreads quickly. That's why I say, without hesitation: politics is cancer. And like cancer, if you don't remove it swiftly and completely, it will destroy everything in its path.

So, why is politics so harmful? The answer is simple: it's about ego, not progress. It's about people trying to climb the ladder, gain influence, or protect their own status, rather than working for the good of the company. When individuals begin to prioritise their own position over the success of the organisation, it creates division. And division leads to inefficiency, mistrust, and ultimately failure. Just like a disease, politics is contagious. If one person starts playing political games, others soon follow, and before long, the entire culture is infected.

UNDERSTANDING POLITICS IN BUSINESS

Politics, in the context of business, is not just disagreements or differences of opinion. Healthy debate is essential for any thriving organisation. But when the focus shifts from ideas and solutions to power and influence, that's when the problems begin. You see this in companies where favouritism rules, where information is withheld to control the narrative, or where people engage in backstabbing and blame-shifting to make themselves look better at the expense of others.

Consider a situation I faced at Success Tutoring. In the early days, a small group of senior tutors formed a close-knit circle, and they began receiving special treatment from a middle manager. These tutors were always given the best-paying jobs, the most desirable students, and the most flexible schedules. Meanwhile, the newer tutors, who were just as skilled and hardworking, felt they were being overlooked. It didn't take long before morale dropped. The new tutors felt discouraged, and their performance suffered. Why? Because no matter how hard they worked, they felt they couldn't compete with the favouritism that was running rampant.

This was politics in its purest form – people using relationships and influence, rather than merit, to get ahead. And the result? Division, resentment, and underperformance. I knew I had to step in, so we made a clear decision: merit would rule. We implemented a system where assignments were based on performance and feedback, not relationships. We ensured that every tutor had an equal opportunity to work with top students. Almost immediately, morale improved. The tutors saw that hard work would be recognised, and that personal relationships held no sway in the decision-making process. The favouritism stopped, and the business grew stronger as a result.

This is the kind of toxic behaviour I refer to when I say "politics is cancer". It starts small – perhaps a subtle favouritism or a quiet back-channel conversation. But if you allow it to spread, it undermines everything you're trying to build. The focus shifts from collaboration and excellence to survival and self-preservation. When employees are more focused on protecting themselves than achieving shared goals, the company's progress grinds to a halt.

WHY POLITICS IS PARTICULARLY HARMFUL IN FRANCHISING

In the world of franchising, politics is even more dangerous. Traditional franchise models often have layers of management and bureaucracy that leave franchise partners feeling like they're trapped in the same hierarchical structure they were trying to escape when they left their 9-to-5 jobs. In these systems, franchise partners report to regional managers, divisional franchisors, and corporate leadership, each with their own agenda. The result? A power struggle, with franchise partners feeling like they have to play the game to succeed rather than focusing on building a great business.

This is why Success Tutoring is built on a flat franchising model. We don't need layers of management. We empower our franchise partners to take charge of their businesses. We give them the tools, the training, and the support they need – but we don't micromanage them. By removing unnecessary hierarchy, we eliminate the need for political manoeuvering. In our system, ideas win – not titles, not relationships, not influence. If you've got a great idea that will help students succeed, that's what matters. Your position means nothing; your execution means everything.

By keeping the structure flat, we allow franchise partners to innovate, lead, and build without feeling like they have to navigate internal politics. This is the future of franchising – where leaders are free to lead and success is based on performance, not political gamesmanship.

THE WARNING SIGNS OF POLITICS

So how do you know when politics is starting to take root in your business? It often starts with small behaviours that are easy to overlook. Here are a few signs to watch for:

1. **Favouritism:** When employees are promoted or rewarded based on relationships rather than performance.
2. **Backstabbing:** When team members undermine each other, either by spreading gossip or subtly sabotaging one another's work.
3. **Withholding Information:** When key employees keep valuable information to themselves in order to maintain control over projects.
4. **Blame Shifting:** When something goes wrong, instead of taking responsibility, employees point fingers to protect themselves.
5. **Cliques:** When small groups form within the organisation that exclude others and make decisions behind closed doors.

These behaviours may seem small at first, but they are the early signs of a much larger problem. If left unchecked, they will spread through the organisation, creating division and resentment. And before long, the focus will shift from progress to protection – from achieving shared goals to personal survival.

HOW TO ELIMINATE POLITICS

At Success Tutoring, we've taken a hardline approach to eliminating politics. For us, it starts with hiring the right people. We don't just hire for skill – we hire for character. We want people who align with our values and who are committed to the company's mission, not their own personal gain. We pick people who believe in collaboration, openness, and transparency. People who thrive in a meritocratic environment where the best ideas win, regardless of who presents them.

Transparency is also key. Open communication helps eliminate the need for back-channel conversations or manipulation. When decisions are made openly and fairly, and when everyone is given the same access to information, politics has no room to grow. At Success Tutoring, we make sure that decisions are based on clear, transparent criteria, so that no one feels like they're being left out of the loop. This keeps everyone focused on the mission rather than on playing political games.

Leadership is also critical in keeping politics at bay. As a leader, you have to be vigilant. You have to lead by example. If your team sees you engaging in political behaviour – playing favourites, withholding information, or undermining others – they will follow suit. But if they see you promoting fairness, rewarding merit, and encouraging collaboration, they will do the same.

At Success Tutoring, I make it a point to call out political behaviour as soon as I see it. I don't allow it to fester. Whether it's a subtle comment made behind someone's back, or a more overt form of favouritism, I address it head-on. And I encourage my managers to do the same. We don't tolerate politics. And as a result, we have a team that's focused on growth, collaboration, and execution – not on protecting their own interests.

THE COST OF POLITICS

The cost of politics is enormous. It saps the energy of your team, destroys morale, and reduces productivity. When people are spending their time trying to navigate political waters, they're not spending it on innovation, problem-solving, or customer service. It slows down decision-making, because people are more concerned with how a decision will affect their personal standing than with what's best for the company.

But perhaps most damaging of all, politics drives away good people. Talented employees – those who are focused on doing great work – don't want to waste their time in a political environment. They want to be recognised for their contributions, not for their ability to play the game. And when they see that politics is valued over merit, they leave. They go somewhere where their talent is appreciated and where they can thrive without navigating personal agendas.

POSITIONS MEAN NOTHING. IDEAS MEAN EVERYTHING.

If you want to succeed – whether as a business owner, a franchisee, or a leader – you need to create an environment where politics cannot survive. That means leading by example, promoting transparency, and ensuring that your team is focused on the mission, not their own personal agendas. It means hiring people with integrity and building a culture where the best ideas win, regardless of who brings them to the table.

Remember this: positions mean nothing. Ideas mean everything.

Politics is cancer. And just like cancer, the only way to stop it is to remove it completely. When you create a business free from politics, you create a business where innovation thrives, where your team is motivated.

CHAPTER 10

POVERTY IS A MINDSET

Poverty is not just a state of financial hardship; it's a state of mind. It reaches beyond money into every area of your life – your health, your relationships, your spirituality, and how you spend your time. If you have a poor mindset, you will always experience lack, no matter how much money you have in the bank. But if you can shift your mindset, you will experience abundance in every area of your life. The truth is, if you fix your mind, you will not have poverty. You will transition from scarcity to abundance. This is the foundation of success, and it applies to everyone, in every situation.

Take a simple challenge. Ask two people you meet the same three questions:
1. What is your name?
2. Tell me about yourself.
3. How did you get here?

Ask these questions to two very different individuals: one homeless person and one person in a suit walking down the street. You will hear contrasting answers. The homeless person will likely talk about the negative things that have happened to them – the circumstances that have led them to where they are now. They may talk about hardships, bad luck, or how the world has been unfair to them. The person in the suit, however, will likely focus on their accomplishments, the opportunities they've taken advantage of, and their goals for the future.

Both of these individuals are living in the same world, but they see it through entirely different lenses. One views life as a series of limitations, the other sees it as filled with possibility. Their external circumstances are different, but those circumstances are largely a reflection of their internal mindset. The world is not a window; it's a mirror. What you see and experience in life is a reflection of your own mindset.

This is why it's essential to develop an abundance mindset, rather than a poverty mindset. Unfortunately, I've seen too many people trapped in poverty not because of a lack of opportunity, but because of the words they say about themselves, and the beliefs they hold deep within. I've volunteered for over ten years, and I've seen time and time again how people's own beliefs keep them stuck in the same place. Poverty is not just financial – it's a mindset.

SHIFTING THE MINDSET

What holds people back in life, keeping them stuck in a poverty mindset? It's not a lack of money, resources, or opportunities. It's the belief that they are not good enough, that they are not worthy of success. These limiting beliefs often stem from childhood, when people are told by family members, teachers, or society that they will never achieve much in life. Over time, these beliefs become ingrained, and people stop believing in themselves. They settle for less than they're capable of.

To shift from a poverty mindset to an abundance mindset, you have to stop making excuses. Excuses are the comfort zone of the poverty mindset. People stuck in poverty come up with reasons why they can't achieve their goals, rather than looking for solutions. It's time to stop complaining, stop waiting for someone to give you permission, and start executing like a hungry lion that won't stop until they've achieved their destiny.

If you want to break free from the limitations you've placed on yourself, you have to grab life by the horns. You cannot settle for second best. You have to make the decision that you are going to push forwards, regardless of what others say or what challenges come your way. Surround yourself with people who have a growth mindset, and cut out the negativity from your life. If someone has a poor mindset and isn't willing to change, they have no place in your life.

A strong, growth-oriented mindset is one of the most powerful tools you can have. With it, you can achieve anything. Without it, you will always feel like something is missing, no matter how much you achieve.

POVERTY VS ABUNDANCE MINDSET

The difference between a poverty mindset and an abundance mindset can be summed up in a few simple words. A poverty mindset says, "I have less, I am less, I am not worthy." It's rooted in scarcity, fear, and the belief that there's never enough to go around. An abundance mindset, on the other hand, says, "I have more, I deserve more, I am worthy." It's rooted in confidence, optimism, and the belief that opportunities are limitless.

Your mindset creates your reality. If you believe in scarcity, you will live in scarcity. If you believe in abundance, you will create abundance. This applies to everything – from your relationships and career, to your finances and health. All aspiring businesspeople must adopt an abundance mindset if they want to thrive. Without it, success will always seem just out of reach.

ESCAPE VELOCITY – BREAKING FREE FROM THE 9-TO-5 ORBIT

Just like a rocket needs immense energy to break free from Earth's gravity, individuals trapped in the corporate 9-to-5 grind must generate enough momentum to escape the pull of their current reality. This concept, known as escape velocity, is essential for anyone striving to achieve financial freedom and build a life of purpose through entrepreneurship.

To achieve escape velocity, you need three critical components:

1. Fuel – Savings and Financial Readiness

Fuel represents your financial preparedness. Just as a rocket needs fuel to power its journey, you need savings or a financial cushion to support your transition. This fuel provides the security to take calculated risks and invest in your side hustle without fear of immediate financial failure.

Tip: Start by building a savings buffer to cover essential expenses for at least six months. This will give you the confidence to take bold steps in your tutoring business.

2. Thrust – Action and Execution in the Tutoring Business

Thrust is the force that propels the rocket upward. In the context of escaping your corporate job, thrust represents your action and execution in building your tutoring business. It's not enough to have ideas – you need to take consistent, deliberate actions to create momentum.

Tip: Focus on income-generating activities (IGAs) that directly contribute to growing your business. This includes acquiring new students, improving your services, and optimising your marketing efforts.

3. Trajectory – Clear Milestones for Revenue and Growth

A rocket needs a clear trajectory to reach space, and your side hustle needs defined milestones to ensure steady progress. Trajectory involves setting specific revenue and growth goals that will guide your journey from part-time hustle to full-time freedom.

Tip: Set short-term, mid-term, and long-term goals. For example:
- **Short-term:** Secure your first ten students.

- **Mid-term:** Generate enough income to replace 50% of your corporate salary.
- **Long-term:** Achieve full income replacement and financial independence.

THE FREEDOM ZONE

Once you achieve escape velocity, you enter the Freedom Zone – a space where you are no longer bound by the constraints of a 9-to-5 job. In this zone, you have the autonomy to shape your future, pursue your passions, and live life on your own terms. The key to reaching this zone is consistent action, financial readiness, and a clear vision of where you're headed.

As entrepreneur Chris Guillebeau once said, *"The most important moment in a side hustle is when it stops being a hobby and starts being a calling."* Achieving escape velocity is the turning point where your tutoring business transforms from a dream into a life-changing reality.

HOW MINDSET AFFECTS WEALTH CREATION

The way you think about money directly affects how much wealth you create. Some people are programmed to think like employees, while others are programmed to think like employers. Which one are you? If you're reading this book, I imagine you want to be an employer. And if that's the case, you must think differently from those who work for others.

Employees trade their time for money. Employers trade value for wealth. This is a key mindset shift that will unlock new opportunities for you. If you have a poor mindset, you will continue to think like an employee, focusing on how much time you put into something. But to build wealth, you must shift your focus to the value you create. Wealth comes from providing value to others, not just from clocking in hours.

This mindset shift is essential if you want to break free from the limitations of an employee's life and become a successful entrepreneur. Focus on how you can serve others, how you can solve problems, and how you can create value. When you do this, wealth will follow.

BREAKING GENERATIONAL POVERTY

Generational poverty is passed down from one generation to the next, not through genetics, but through mindset. If your family never owned a business or struggled financially, there's a good chance you inherited a poverty mindset without even realising it. Breaking free from generational poverty requires you to reprogram your mind. You must unlearn the limiting beliefs that have been passed down to you and replace them with new, empowering beliefs.

Many families instill a scarcity mindset in their children by saying things like, "Money doesn't grow on trees." This teaches children that wealth is hard to come by, and it conditions them to accept financial struggle as a normal part of life. To break free from generational poverty, you must challenge these beliefs and adopt a mindset of abundance. You must believe that wealth is available to you and that you are capable of achieving it.

Mentorship and self-improvement are crucial in this process. Surround yourself with people who have already achieved the success you want. Learn from their experiences, absorb their mindset, and apply their lessons to your own life. This is how you reprogram your mind and break free from the limitations of your upbringing.

THE POWER OF ENVIRONMENT

Your environment plays a huge role in shaping your mindset. The family you were born into, the society you grew up in, and the people you spend time with all influence how you think. If you grew up in an environment where financial struggle was common, it's easy to adopt a poverty mindset without even realising it.

But just because you were raised in that environment doesn't mean you're stuck there. You can change your mindset by changing your environment. Surround yourself with people who have an abundance mindset. Read books, listen to podcasts, and consume content that challenges you to think bigger. When you expose yourself to new ideas and positive influences, you begin to shift your thinking.

Many of the franchise partners in Success Tutoring come from backgrounds where business ownership was never part of their reality. For these individuals, mindset is everything. The transition from employee to business owner requires a complete shift in thinking. But once that shift happens, the possibilities are endless.

DAILY HABITS FOR AN ABUNDANCE MINDSET

Building an abundance mindset doesn't happen overnight. It requires daily habits and consistent effort. One of the most powerful tools for shifting your mindset is goal setting. When you set clear goals for yourself, you give your mind a target to focus on. This helps you stay on track and maintain a positive mindset, even when challenges arise.

Another powerful tool is creating a vision board. A vision board is a collection of images that represent the life you want to create. By looking at it every day, you keep your goals at the forefront of your mind. Visualisation is another technique that can help you shift from a poverty mindset to an abundance mindset. Spend time each day visualising the life you want to live. Picture yourself achieving your goals, living in abundance, and experiencing success.

The more vividly you can imagine it, the more real it will become.

Finally, daily affirmations are essential. What you say to yourself shapes your beliefs. If you repeatedly tell yourself, "I am successful, I am wealthy, I am worthy," you will start to believe it. Over time, these positive affirmations will replace the negative self-talk that has been holding you back.

OVERCOMING LIMITING BELIEFS

Limiting beliefs are the chains that hold people back. They say things like, "I'm not good enough," "I don't have enough resources," or "I'll start once I have more money." These beliefs are rooted in fear, and they keep people trapped in mediocrity. To break free, you must identify these limiting beliefs and replace them with empowering ones.

When I first started Success Tutoring, I made a lot of money in a short period of time. People around me, who had no business experience, told me to save the money. But I had a different mindset. Instead of saving, I invested everything I had into opening a second location. That decision was one of the best I've ever made. Had I listened to those with a scarcity mindset, I wouldn't be where I am today. By taking bold action and believing in abundance, I unlocked my full potential as an entrepreneur.

Make the decision now to change your mindset. Put your past behind you and focus on the future. You are capable of more than you realise, but you must first believe it. Cultivate a mindset of abundance, and the world will open up to you. Stop waiting, stop making excuses, and start living the life you were destined for. The only thing standing between you and the life you want is your mindset. Change your mind, and you will change your life.

CHAPTER 11

HAVE THE RIGHT MINDSET

There is undeniable power in positivity. It's not just a feel-good concept; it's a real force that can transform your life from the inside out. The way we think shapes the world we live in, and when we shift our mindset to one of strength and resilience, our entire reality changes.

But positivity isn't something that comes naturally every day. Life challenges us, tests us, and sometimes leaves us questioning why we're even on this path in the first place. Yet, I've found that through every challenge, the mindset I chose became my greatest asset. It was a tool that propelled me forwards when the road seemed too steep to climb.

THE FOUNDATION OF A POSITIVE MINDSET

The most powerful first step in developing a positive mindset is simple: *Believe in yourself.* This belief drives you to take risks, keep pushing forwards, and find solutions instead of giving up. Self-belief is what separates those who give up from those who push on and achieve something extraordinary.

I remember clearly the moment I nearly walked away from this journey. It was late 2022, and I was at a point where I felt defeated. I even wrote an email to Doug, saying, "I'm coming very close to leaving the tutoring business and starting something new...I feel like I'm putting too much work into something that isn't resulting in equal or more reward." I felt like I'd given all I had, and the reward wasn't reflecting the effort.

But, after hitting "send", I took a step back and reminded myself why I began this journey in the first place. I realised that setbacks and frustrations are just part of the process. They don't define the end goal. If anything, they give us the grit and tenacity to push even harder.

The greatest obstacles we face are often the ones in our minds. When you see challenges as temporary, and believe you have what it takes to overcome them, you unlock a level of courage you may not have even known was there.

VISUALISING SUCCESS

Visualisation is another powerful tool for a positive mindset. It's about seeing your dreams and goals clearly, even before they happen. When you visualise success, you start to bring it into your reality. Personally, I'm a big believer in vision boards. They're not just nice to look at – they're daily reminders of where you want to go.

Throughout my journey, I've created vision boards filled with images of my goals. Whether it was a photograph of a successful leader I admire or an image that symbolised the growth I wanted for Success Tutoring, I used those images to keep me focused. I'd look at them every day, allowing them to drive me forwards, even when I felt uninspired. This isn't just about wishing for things; it's about training your mind to see those goals as achievable realities. When you internalise these images, they become part of you. You start working towards them with a renewed sense of purpose.

THE FREEDOM LADDER: A STEP-BY-STEP FRAMEWORK FOR TRANSITIONING FROM CORPORATE TO JOB ENTREPRENEURSHIP

The journey from a corporate job to full-time entrepreneurship isn't a leap of faith – it's a series of calculated steps. The Freedom Ladder provides a structured, actionable framework to guide families – especially dual-income households – through this transition. By following each rung of the ladder, families can achieve financial security, operational stability, and long-term success through a tutoring franchise.

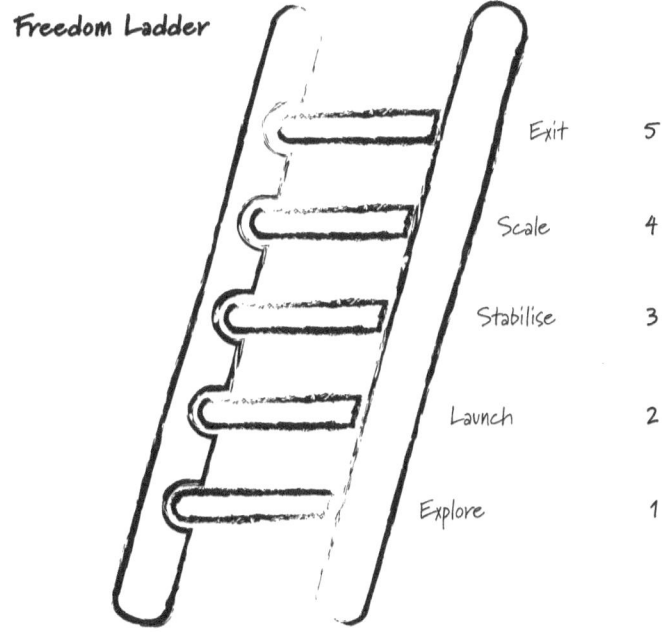

Just like a ladder, each step builds on the one before it, ensuring a gradual and manageable climb towards freedom. Here's how it works:

1. Explore (Rung 1: Discovery Phase)
"Lay the groundwork for your new journey."
In this initial phase, families evaluate whether franchising is the right path for them. It's about understanding motivations, researching the opportunity, and assessing financial readiness.

Steps:
- **Identify Your Why:** Understand your motivations for pursuing a tutoring franchise (e.g., financial freedom, flexibility, impact).
- **Research the Opportunity:** Explore the Success Tutoring franchise model, profitability, and operational requirements.
- **Assess Your Fit:** Use tools like the Franchise Fit Test to determine if you and your spouse are ready for the commitment.
- **Plan Your Budget:** Calculate the initial investment, ongoing expenses, and a financial buffer to ensure security.

Milestone: Decide to move forwards with purchasing a franchise, backed by clear goals and a financial plan.

2. Launch (Rung 2: Launch Phase)
"Start small and build a strong foundation."
This phase focuses on launching the business while maintaining stability. It's often the stage where one spouse works part-time in the franchise while the other maintains a corporate job.

Steps:
- **Complete Training:** Attend the SuccessAcademy to learn the business model, systems, and best practices.
- **Set Up Operations:** Secure your location, hire tutors, and establish your membership-based model.
- **Start Part-Time:** Focus on building the business during available hours while maintaining work-life balance.
- **Market Locally:** Begin building your presence in the community through outreach, referrals, and targeted marketing.

Milestone: Launch your tutoring centre with a manageable number of students to ensure smooth operations and quality service.

3. Stabilise (Rung 3: Growth Phase)
"Achieve consistency in operations and income."
At this stage, the focus shifts to achieving financial stability and refining processes to ensure the business runs smoothly.

Steps:
- **Reach Financial Break-Even:** Cover all operational costs through consistent revenue streams.
- **Optimise Systems:** Streamline day-to-day operations to ensure the franchise runs smoothly without constant oversight.
- **Involve the Husband Part-Time:** The husband can start supporting the franchise during evenings or weekends, focusing on growth areas like marketing or strategic planning.
- **Reinvest in Growth:** Use profits to expand your marketing efforts or invest in technology and staff training.

Milestone: Achieve financial stability where the franchise generates a predictable, surplus income.

4. Scale (Rung 4: Expansion Phase)
"Grow beyond one location to maximise income potential."
Once the business is stable, families can explore scaling opportunities by opening a second location or increasing the capacity of the first.

Steps:
- **Assess Expansion Readiness:** Use tools like the Scalability Scorecard to determine if your first location can sustain growth.
- **Hire a Manager:** Delegate day-to-day responsibilities at the first location to free up time for expansion.
- **Open a Second Site:** Use your experience and resources to launch another tutoring centre in a nearby area.
- **Focus on Leadership:** Both spouses can now transition into higher-level roles overseeing multiple locations.

Milestone: Generate enough revenue from two or more locations to replace the husband's full-time income, setting the stage for him to quit his corporate job.

5. Exit (Rung 5: Freedom Phase)
"Achieve full financial and lifestyle freedom."
The final rung of the ladder is the ultimate goal: full financial freedom and lifestyle flexibility. At this stage, both spouses have transitioned into the business full-time.

Steps:
- **Replace Corporate Salaries:** Ensure the combined revenue from your franchises exceeds your household's previous dual income.

- **Refine Work-Life Balance:** Adjust roles and responsibilities to prioritise family time and personal goals.
- **Plan for Legacy:** Position your business as a long-term asset by building equity or preparing for future sale or transfer.
- **Expand or Diversify:** Consider further scaling the business or exploring complementary ventures like online tutoring or additional franchises.

Milestone: Both spouses have left their corporate jobs, and the tutoring business generates stable, growing income with scalable systems in place.

The Freedom Ladder provides a roadmap for families to escape the corporate grind and build a life of financial independence through entrepreneurship. With each step, the risks are mitigated, and the rewards grow exponentially. It's not just about making money – it's about creating a legacy of freedom, flexibility, and purpose.

TURNING SETBACKS INTO STEPPING STONES

Having a positive mindset isn't about pretending everything is perfect. It's about facing challenges with resilience. Over the years, I've encountered my fair share of setbacks, some bigger than others. There were times when things didn't go according to plan, when financial pressures mounted, or when my team encountered issues that took me by surprise. Every one of those moments tested my resolve, but I chose to keep pushing forwards.

I'll never forget the time during the pandemic when we applied for a government grant to keep the business afloat. I later found out we weren't eligible for it, and we had to pay the money back. I was frustrated, feeling blindsided, and it was a tough moment. But I reminded myself that setbacks are part of the process. If I had let every problem hold me down, I wouldn't be where I am today. Setbacks, after all, are simply opportunities to learn and grow. This is where a positive mindset makes all the difference: it gives you the ability to transform challenges into fuel.

POSITIVE SELF-TALK AND INNER DIALOGUE

What you say to yourself matters more than you might realise. Negative self-talk can become a cycle, draining your confidence and convincing you that you're not capable. I've learned to be conscious of my inner dialogue, especially during difficult times. When things aren't going well, I remind myself of the things I've achieved, of my own strengths, and of the purpose that drives me forwards.

I've even gotten into the habit of speaking to myself with encouragement. There were times when I'd look in the mirror and say, "You've got this. You're stronger than this challenge. You're going to make it through." It might sound strange, but it works. It reinforces my resolve and builds my confidence.

When you tell yourself that you're capable, resilient, and that you have what it takes, you start to believe it. It's a mindset that propels you forwards, even on the tough days. And the truth is, that's what separates those who push through from those who give up.

CHOOSING POSITIVE INFLUENCES

Surrounding yourself with positive influences is key. There's a saying that you're the average of the five people you spend the most time with. Over the years, I've learned how true that is. When I first started out, I realised not everyone around me was aligned with my vision. Some people just couldn't see what I was working towards and, whether intentionally or not, they held me back.

Today, I choose my inner circle carefully. I surround myself with people who believe in me, who push me to reach higher, and who inspire me to keep going. Positivity is contagious. When you're around people who are driven, passionate, and supportive, you start to reflect those qualities in your own life.

THE ROLE OF FAITH IN POSITIVITY

A positive mindset, I believe, is often grounded in faith. I'm not necessarily talking about religious faith, but a belief in something greater than yourself – a belief that your purpose is bigger than the challenges you face. For me, that faith has been an anchor. When I couldn't see the path forwards, I trusted that by staying true to my purpose, the way would eventually become clear.

Faith gives you the courage to take risks, to keep pushing, and to know that setbacks are part of a bigger plan. It's about trusting that things will work out in the end, even if it's not obvious right now. That's the faith that allows me to persevere, no matter what comes my way.

STEPS FOR BUILDING A POSITIVE MINDSET

Here are a few steps that have helped me build a positive mindset over the years:

1. **Start Every Day with Gratitude**
   Take a few minutes each morning to reflect on things you're grateful for. This sets a positive tone for the day and keeps you focused on the good.
2. **Create a Vision Board**
   Fill your board with images that represent your goals. This keeps your aspirations front and centre and serves as a daily reminder of what you're working towards.

3. **Practice Positive Self-Talk**
   Be mindful of the way you speak to yourself. Replace doubt with affirmations that reinforce your capabilities and strengths.
4. **Surround Yourself with Positivity**
   Choose to spend time with people who support you, encourage you, and push you to be your best self.
5. **Trust the Process**
   Have faith in your journey. Remember that every setback is just a setup for a comeback. Trust that the challenges you face are part of the process.
6. **Visualise Success**
   Spend a few minutes each day visualising your goals. Imagine yourself achieving them. Feel the emotions, see the details, and make it real in your mind.
7. **Turn Challenges into Opportunities**
   When faced with a setback, ask yourself, "What can I learn from this?" Use every challenge as a chance to grow stronger.

IT IS YOUR CHOICE

Positivity is a choice we make every day. It's about choosing to see challenges as temporary, believing in yourself, and trusting that you have the power to create the life you want. When I look back on my journey, I can see that my mindset has been my greatest asset. It has carried me through the toughest times and kept me focused on my vision.

Remember, you have the power to shape your reality. Your thoughts, beliefs, and attitude are the foundation of your success. Embrace positivity, and let it guide you to a life filled with purpose, resilience, and fulfilment.

FROM TEACHER TO INVESTOR: SHIFTING MINDSET, TRANSFORMING LIVES

Sam, Success Tutoring Chermside, QLD

For over a decade, I dedicated my life to teaching. As a high school teacher, I loved working with students and helping them reach their potential. But over time, I realised that while I was making an impact in the classroom, I was also stuck in a system that limited my growth. I had dreams of doing something bigger – something that would allow me to make a broader impact on my community while creating more freedom for myself and my family.

That's when I discovered Success Tutoring. The franchise wasn't just another business opportunity – it represented a mindset shift. It showed me that if I wanted to change my life, I had to start by changing my perspective. I had to move from thinking like an employee to thinking like an investor and entrepreneur.

The Success Tutoring model aligned perfectly with my values as an educator. The focus wasn't just on improving grades; it was about motivating, inspiring, and uplifting students to unlock their full potential. That philosophy resonated deeply with me. I realised that by becoming a franchise owner, I could continue doing what I loved – helping students thrive – while also building a business that would secure my family's future.

One of the most important lessons I've learned through this journey is that success begins with the right mindset. Making the leap from teacher to business owner wasn't easy. There were moments of doubt and fear, but I kept reminding myself that growth happens outside of your comfort zone. I had to trust the process, follow the Success Tutoring systems, and believe in my ability to succeed.

When we launched Success Tutoring Chermside, we welcomed over 70 students from day one. It was a testament to the demand for quality, personalised education in our community. Seeing students grow academically and gain confidence has been one of the most fulfilling experiences of my life. I've gone from being a teacher in a classroom to a community leader, making a lasting impact on families in our area.

The systems and support provided by SuccessAcademy have been invaluable. As someone new to business ownership, I appreciated the clear processes, training, and ongoing mentorship. I wasn't just starting a business – I was joining a network of like-minded individuals who shared the same passion for education and personal development.

Now, as a franchise owner, I've achieved something I never thought possible – I've created a life of freedom, flexibility, and purpose. I'm no longer bound by the restrictions of a traditional teaching career. Instead, I'm building a legacy for my family and empowering students to achieve their dreams.

For teachers considering a career change, my advice is simple: have the right mindset. Success isn't about taking the safest path – it's about taking the path that aligns with your values and vision. If you're willing to step outside your comfort zone, embrace a new way of thinking, and trust in a proven system, the rewards are life-changing.

Joining Success Tutoring has been one of the best decisions of my life. I'm building a thriving business, impacting my community, and living a life of purpose. If you're ready to make a real difference – for yourself and for others – this is your opportunity.

CHAPTER 12

EVERYTHING YOU KNOW ABOUT BUSINESS IS WRONG

When it comes to business, there are so many misconceptions that hold people back from realising their potential. For most of us, we've been conditioned to think a certain way about business, to believe certain "truths" that are nothing more than stereotypes and myths. These misconceptions can create fear, paralyse progress, and make business seem like a distant dream, only accessible to a select few. But the reality is that everything you've been told about business is probably wrong.

In this chapter, I want to dispel some of the most common business myths, debunk the preconceived ideas people have, and give you a new perspective on what it really takes to be successful in business. I've built my own business from the ground up and encountered all kinds of misinformation along the way. The truth is, business isn't as complicated or out of reach as most people make it out to be – if you approach it with the right mindset and understanding.

MYTH #1: YOU NEED A LOT OF MONEY TO START A BUSINESS

One of the biggest misconceptions people have is that you need a huge amount of capital to start a business. They think that unless you have investors lined up or you've saved a fortune, you can't even begin to think about entrepreneurship. This couldn't be further from the truth.

I started Success Tutoring with just $250. It was all I had, but I invested it in some simple marketing materials – car magnets, posters, and a Facebook page. That $250 laid the foundation for what has become one of the largest tutoring franchises in Australia. The key wasn't how much money I had; it was how resourceful I could be with what I had. Too often, people think lack of money is the reason they can't start, but it's not about resources – it's about resourcefulness.

MYTH #2: BUSINESS IS RISKY AND MOST FAIL

Yes, you've probably heard it before – "most businesses fail in the first year". It's one of those common sayings that discourages countless people from even trying. But let's put this into perspective. The reason most businesses fail is not because business itself is risky, but because the people running them are either misinformed, underprepared, or simply not executing well. Success in business comes down to strategy, support, and persistence, not the myth of inherent risk.

If you believe the statistics about failure, then of course, you'll never start. But here's something most people don't know: if you start a franchise, like Success Tutoring, your chances of success increase dramatically. Why? Because franchises come with a proven model, a support system, and a guide to execution. In fact, franchise businesses have a 90% higher chance of success compared to traditional startups.

It's not that business is risky – it's that people need the right tools and mindset to reduce the risk.

MYTH #3: BUSINESS OWNERS DON'T HAVE PERSONAL LIVES

There's this image that to be a successful business owner, you have to sacrifice everything – your personal life, your relationships, your hobbies. People think you have to work 24/7 and live in a constant state of stress. This stereotype makes entrepreneurship seem unattainable for anyone who values their personal time.

But here's the reality: business ownership gives you freedom. When you set up your business properly, hire the right people, and implement systems, you can create more time for the things you love. When I started Success Tutoring, I was able to build a business that not only allowed me to do something I was passionate about but also gave me the freedom to spend time with my family, travel, and enjoy life. The idea that business owners must give up everything is outdated. With the right approach, you can have both – a successful business and a fulfilling personal life.

MYTH #4: YOU NEED TO INVENT SOMETHING NEW TO SUCCEED

Some people think that to succeed in business, you need to come up with a groundbreaking, never-before-seen idea. They believe that unless you're the next Elon Musk or Steve Jobs, your business won't have a chance. But let me tell you, the success of your business has nothing to do with the novelty of your idea. It's about how you execute that idea.

Look at my business, Success Tutoring. I didn't invent tutoring. I didn't create some brand-new educational method. What I did was improve on what already existed. I focused on motivating, inspiring, and uplifting students, creating a culture of success, and providing a service that parents could trust. The idea wasn't revolutionary – the execution was. Success isn't about what you come up with, but how well you bring it to life.

MYTH #5: IF YOUR IDEA IS GOOD, SUCCESS IS GUARANTEED

On the flip side, some people think that if they have a brilliant idea, success is inevitable. They believe that the idea is everything and that as long as the concept is solid, everything else will fall into place. This is another dangerous misconception. Your idea, no matter how great, is worthless without execution.

I've seen people with fantastic ideas fail miserably because they didn't know how to market them, build the right team, or create systems to scale. An idea is just the starting point. The real work – the part that guarantees success – is in how you bring that idea to the market, how you solve problems, how you adapt, and how you execute.

MYTH #6: YOU HAVE TO TAKE HUGE RISKS TO MAKE IT BIG

Another myth that holds people back is the belief that to make it big in business, you have to take massive risks. People think you need to put everything on the line, gamble with your life savings, or take out enormous loans to stand a chance of succeeding. But the truth is, smart business owners don't take reckless risks – they take calculated ones.

When I started Success Tutoring, I didn't jump into a high-risk situation without thinking. I took small, manageable steps. I tested the market, reinvested my profits, and grew the business strategically. The idea isn't to risk everything – it's to take the right steps, minimise your exposure, and build your business in a way that allows you to grow steadily.

Taking unnecessary risks won't get you there any faster – in fact, it could derail your progress.

THE RIGHT WAY TO THINK ABOUT BUSINESS

So, if everything you know about business is wrong, what's the right way to think about it? For starters, you need to shift your mindset. Business is not about having the perfect idea, working yourself to death, or taking massive risks. It's about execution, strategy, and persistence. It's about building something that aligns with your passion and gives you the freedom to live the life you want.

When you approach business with the right mindset, you begin to see opportunities where others see obstacles. You stop being paralysed by fear and start seeing challenges as stepping stones to success. You realise that business isn't about reinventing the wheel – it's about improving what's already there and executing it better than anyone else.

REAL-WORLD LESSONS

Take my journey with Success Tutoring. I didn't have a lot of money, I didn't invent something new, and I wasn't taking huge risks. But what I did have was a clear vision, a passion for helping students, and a determination to execute that vision in a way that made a difference. I worked smart, not hard, and I surrounded myself with a team that shared my values and commitment.

And that's how business should be. It's not about following the myths that society has conditioned us to believe – it's about breaking free from those misconceptions and creating something that works for you.

RIGHT MINDSET = SUCCESS

If you take anything away from this chapter, let it be this: don't let the myths about business hold you back. You don't need to be rich, take massive risks, or work yourself to the bone to succeed. What you need is the right mindset, the right approach, and the willingness to execute. Everything else is just noise. So, block out the stereotypes, focus on what really matters, and go build the business – and the life – you deserve.

CHAPTER 13

FINDING YOUR PASSION

Passion. It's that fire that burns deep within us, urging us to strive for more, to push boundaries, to leave our mark on the world. Yet, how many people truly live a life driven by passion? How many of us have been lulled into believing that life is meant to be safe, predictable, and mundane? If you're reading this, it's time to change your perspective. It's time to break free from the mold and start pursuing the life you were destined for. But before we delve deeper, let me share one fundamental truth with you: everyone has a purpose. Whether you believe in God, the universe, or some higher power, one thing is certain – you have a gift, a unique reason for being here.

DEFINING PASSION

What is passion? For me, passion is that thing you wake up excited about, the thing that fuels you to work even when no one is watching. It's not just something you stumble upon. It's something you discover over time by trying new things, testing your limits, and embracing failures along the way. Everyone has a passion inside of them. It's not a question of "if" but "when" you will find it. And once you do, it transforms everything.

We are not here to live ordinary lives. Each of us has a calling, a specific talent, a unique purpose that can change the world. Some people are meant to sing, others are born to build businesses, others to become doctors, teachers, or engineers. The challenge is finding that calling. You have to step out of your comfort zone and try as many things as possible until you uncover what lights that spark within you.

One thing I want to stress is this: you will not find your passion by going with the flow. Most people settle into jobs they aren't passionate about, going through the motions without realising the time they are wasting. You have two choices in life – live to the fullest or go with the flow. And let me tell you, when you choose to live to the fullest, magic happens. When you follow your heart (or your intuition, or whatever you call it), you are aligned with your true potential and purpose.

DISCOVERING PASSION

Some people say, "But how do I find my passion?" The answer is simple: explore. Step into the unknown. If you're unsure of your path, try as many things as possible until you find what you love. Passion isn't something that arrives with certainty from day one. It takes curiosity, effort, and persistence to find what resonates with your soul. I believe that everyone has a passion. However, the sad truth is that most people don't find it. Don't be one of those people. Don't let fear or excuses keep you from pursuing what truly fulfils you.

A lot of times, people let external pressures – society, family, or even their own limiting beliefs – convince them that their passion isn't "realistic". They settle for jobs that pay the bills, rather than chasing their dreams. But the reality is, if you're not passionate about what you're doing, what's the point? Life is too short to spend it doing something that doesn't set your soul on fire.

THE PASSION COMPASS

Finding your passion isn't just about following what excites you – it's about aligning your passion with purpose and practicality. The Passion Compass is a powerful tool designed to guide individuals towards a fulfilling career by integrating what they love, what the world needs, what they're good at, and what they can get paid for. Think of it as your personal roadmap to discovering your *True North*.

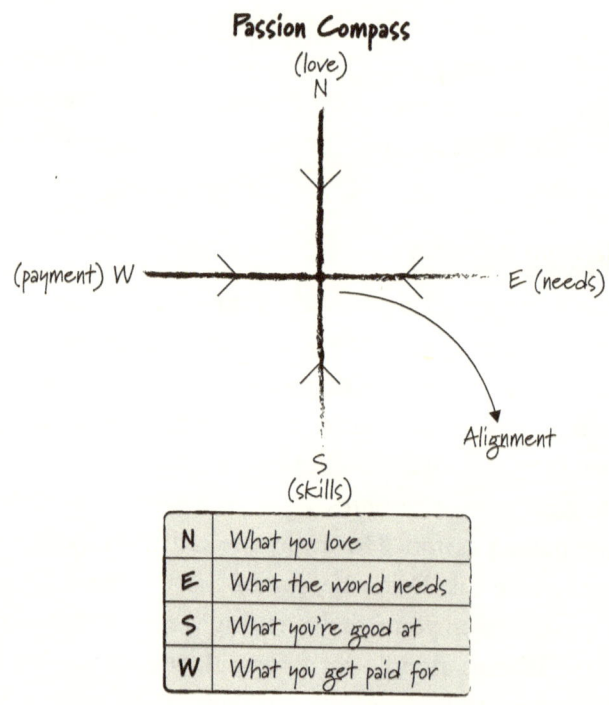

The Passion Compass is modeled like a traditional compass, with four cardinal points representing key elements to explore and balance:
- N (North) – What You Love
- E (East) – What the World Needs
- S (South) – What You're Good At
- W (West) – What You Can Get Paid For

When these four elements align, you find yourself at the centre point – your True North – where passion, purpose, and practicality converge to form a fulfilling and sustainable career path.

HOW THE PASSION COMPASS WORKS

The Passion Compass invites self-reflection in four key areas:

N (North) – What You Love

This quadrant represents your natural interests, hobbies, and activities that energise you. It's the spark that makes you lose track of time and keeps you motivated.

Questions to Reflect On:
- What activities make you lose track of time?
- What topics do you find yourself gravitating towards in conversations?
- What would you do even if you weren't paid for it?

E (East) – What the World Needs

This quadrant encourages you to think about how your passion can meet a broader societal or market need. It's about solving problems and making a difference.

Questions to Reflect On:
- What problems in the world or community do you feel compelled to solve?
- How can your skills and passions contribute to improving lives?
- Are there unmet needs in the industry or field that excite you?

S (South) – What You're Good At

Here, you focus on your talents, skills, and areas of expertise. Identifying what you excel at can help you build confidence and find ways to contribute meaningfully.

Questions to Reflect On:
- What have you been praised for in the past?
- What skills come naturally to you?
- What do others ask you for help with?

W (West) – What You Can Get Paid For

This quadrant focuses on financial sustainability. It's about finding ways to monetise your passion so that it becomes a viable career path.

Questions to Reflect On:
- What career paths or business ideas align with your skills and passions?
- What services or products are people willing to pay you for?
- Are there trends or opportunities in the market related to your passion?

PRACTICAL APPLICATION OF THE PASSION COMPASS

The Passion Compass isn't just a theory – it's a practical tool that can be applied step-by-step to map out your career journey:

1. **Brainstorm in Each Quadrant:**
   - Write down your answers to the reflection questions for each direction (N, E, S, W).
2. **Find Patterns:**
   - Look for overlaps where your answers align across multiple quadrants. For example:
     - If you love teaching (North), are good at explaining concepts (South), see a need for better education tools (East), and can monetise through tutoring (West), then tutoring might be your aligned passion.
3. **Map Your Alignment:**
   - The centre point, where all four elements intersect, represents your True North – your aligned passion and purpose.

EXAMPLE OF THE PASSION COMPASS IN ACTION

Imagine a person who:
- **N:** Loves cooking and experimenting with recipes.
- **E:** Sees a need for healthier meal options for busy families.
- **S:** Is skilled at meal prep and creating easy-to-follow recipes.
- **W:** Can monetise by starting a meal delivery service or selling a cookbook.

Their Passion Compass points towards creating a healthy meal delivery service that combines their love for cooking, their skill set, and a market need, while also being financially sustainable.

WHY THE PASSION COMPASS WORKS

The Passion Compass avoids the trap of focusing on passion in isolation. Too often, people are told to simply "follow their passion" without considering whether it's practical or aligned with what the world needs. The Passion Compass ensures that your chosen path is both fulfilling and sustainable by incorporating practicality (skills and payment) and purpose (solving real-world needs).

At Success Tutoring, we encourage our tutors and franchise partners to use the Passion Compass as a guiding framework. Whether you're figuring out your next career move or refining your business focus, this tool can help you stay on course towards your True North.

The Passion Compass isn't just about finding what you love – it's about creating a life where passion and purpose intersect with practicality and impact.

OVERCOMING OBSTACLES TO FINDING PASSION

One of the biggest obstacles to finding your passion is the limiting beliefs we impose on ourselves. How many times have you heard people say, "It's too expensive to start a business" or "I don't have the time"? These are just excuses, roadblocks we create in our minds to stay within our comfort zones. To find your passion, you must first believe that you have a purpose and that you are worthy of pursuing it.

Your passion may not be to work a 9-to-5 job. In fact, I believe that most people are not meant to live that kind of life. You need to ask yourself: "Am I following my purpose, or am I simply doing what I'm told?" I strongly believe that anyone can have a business, but it must be aligned with their passion. When you follow your passion, you create something that serves both you and the world around you.

Another common hurdle is societal or familial expectations. How many people have given up on their dreams because they were told they were unrealistic? How many people let go of what they truly wanted because it didn't fit the mold society placed on them? I've seen it time and time again. But don't be one of those people. The only opinion that matters is yours. At the end of the day, you are the one living your life, and you must be true to yourself.

TURNING PASSION INTO SUCCESS

When you find your passion, everything changes. People can feel your energy, your excitement, and your commitment. They are drawn to you because they can see that you love what you do. In my own journey with Success Tutoring, it wasn't just about tutoring. It was about creating a business that motivated, inspired, and uplifted others. That was my passion. And because I loved what I did, the business thrived.

But finding your passion is just the first step. Turning it into a profitable venture is the next. My advice to those who have found their passion but don't know how to make it profitable? Find a franchise or business model that aligns with your purpose. Learn the system, and apply your passion to it. When you're passionate, success follows.

ALIGNING PASSION WITH PURPOSE

Passion and purpose go hand in hand. When you find your passion, you find purpose in life. And when you have purpose, you will stop at nothing to achieve your goals. For example, when COVID-19 hit, and I had my first two franchise partners, it would have been easy to give up. But I had a passion for what I was doing, and that passion kept me going. Despite the challenges, I stayed focused, determined to provide value to my franchise partners.

That's what passion does. It gives you the strength to push through the obstacles. It keeps you grounded when things get tough. If I didn't love what I did, I would have quit long ago. But passion is what keeps me working, what keeps me building, what keeps me striving to create the best tutoring system in the world.

PRACTICAL ADVICE FOR READERS

So, if you're reading this and haven't found your passion yet, start exploring. Try new things, take risks, and don't be afraid to fail. The path to finding your passion is not always easy, but it's worth it. And once you find it, hold onto it with everything you've got.

If you already know what your passion is, but you're facing challenges, remember this: don't think about your 9-to-5 job. Focus on building something that aligns with your passion. Your passion will carry you through the hard times.

PERSONAL STORY

I've faced many challenges on my journey, but one of the toughest was during COVID-19. At the time, Success Tutoring was growing, but we faced enormous setbacks. We had received government grants to support the business, but months later, we were told we had to refund over $100,000. At the time, I didn't have the money, and it felt like the business was about to collapse. But I didn't give up. I fought through it, wrote a 30-page report to the government, and explained the situation. The lesson I learned? Always have the right advisors around you, and never give up when you're passionate about what you do.

FOLLOW YOUR PASSION AT ALL COSTS

At the end of the day, my message is this: follow your passion at all costs. You only have one life, and it's too precious to waste on something you don't love. Don't let fear, societal expectations, or limiting beliefs hold you back. Pursue your passion with everything you've got, and the success will follow.

Passion is what makes life worth living. It's what drives us to achieve greatness. When you find your passion, you'll find your purpose. And when you find your purpose, you'll find fulfilment beyond anything you've ever imagined.

As you go forwards, remember this: follow your passion. You only have one life to live. Make it count.

PART 3

BUSINESS STRATEGIES & GROWTH

CHAPTER 14

THE SECRET SAUCE TO SUCCESS

There's this notion floating around that success can be boiled down to a single, elusive secret. I'm here to tell you there's no secret. The truth is, no formula, no quick fix, and no silver bullet will make you successful overnight. Success is something you earn, step by step, through hard work, resilience, and a lot of heart. But if there's one thing I'd say is my "secret sauce", it's this: think big.

Thinking big is a critical habit, and I believe it's one of the most powerful tools you can carry with you on the journey to success. Thinking big means dreaming up possibilities that excite you, challenging what seems possible, and never being afraid to aim high. Thinking big is not about recklessness; it's about believing that you're capable of great things. And when you begin to believe that, you attract those opportunities into your life.

Let me share some stories from my own journey that highlight the power of thinking big. Each of these moments, big and small, reinforced in me that if you have the courage to set your sights high, you can change the course of your life – and maybe even the world.

REACHING OUT TO THE GIANTS

There was a time I reached out to one of the largest education investment groups in the world. Now, let's be clear – there was no guarantee they'd even respond. But that didn't matter to me. I figured, "Why not?" and I took the leap. To my surprise, they replied, and before I knew it, I was on a video call with them. That call led to a series of meetings and detailed conversations about what an investment deal might look like.

After several rounds of discussions, they came to visit some of our locations, and I flew out to their head office to meet with their board of directors. There I was, sitting across the table from four executives who had each run publicly listed companies for over 20 years. These people had managed billions of dollars and countless employees, and yet, here I was, a young entrepreneur from Sydney, sitting with them and discussing the future of my business.

By the end of it, they made me an offer just shy of three million dollars. As tempting as it was, I turned it down because I knew I could take the company further on my own. That deal wasn't meant to be, but the experience showed me the importance of thinking big and reaching out, no matter how ambitious or intimidating it may seem.

RISING TO NEW HEIGHTS

There's nothing like being the youngest person on a panel of seasoned franchise executives. When I joined the Franchise Council of Australia, I was asked to sit on a panel to discuss franchise development. The other panellists were all over 35 and had decades of experience leading major franchise companies. I was only 25, but thinking big had earned me a seat at that table.

It was intimidating, sure, but it was also invigorating. I learned a great deal, and I walked away with the realisation that success isn't measured by age or titles – it's about the impact you're willing to make and the goals you're determined to achieve. Being on that panel made me even more resolute in my ambitions for Success Tutoring. It was a reminder that I was on the right path and that thinking big can place you among giants.

AUSTRALIA'S BEST

When I first started Success Tutoring, I wasn't content with being just another tutoring service. I decided to brand it as "Australia's Best Tutoring" right from the start. I created a stamp that we put on every worksheet and even printed it on our business cards. Did it seem a bit audacious? Maybe. But I knew that if we were going to make a name for ourselves, we needed to start thinking – and acting – like we already were the best.

In those early days, I also bought a world map and put it up in our tiny head office. Then, I placed our logo over Australia. I told the team that one day, we'd cover not just Australia but other countries, too. Today, we're well on our way to becoming a global leader in education, and I often look back at that map as a reminder of how far a little audacity can take you.

INVESTING IN THE BEST

When I started franchising Success Tutoring, I didn't hire the top lawyers straight away. Initially, I worked with a legal team that wasn't necessarily specialised in franchising. They weren't the cheapest, but they weren't the best either.

Once I had a few franchise agreements signed, I knew it was time to step up our game. I reached out to a friend who owned a franchise business, and after some searching, we hired one of the best franchise lawyers in the country.

Choosing to work with top professionals made all the difference. It allowed us to scale with confidence and to have the necessary protections in place. Thinking big means recognising when it's time to invest in the best because when you're aiming high, you can't afford to settle.

BUILDING THE RIGHT CONNECTIONS

Thinking big also means surrounding yourself with people who can help you grow. I once reached out to Mohan Dhall, the founder of the International Tutoring Association. He'd been in education for over 20 years and had built a wealth of knowledge. We met for coffee in Sydney, and he told me about everything his organisation does. I remembered using some of the resources he had developed when I was in high school, and here I was, talking business with him over coffee.

Mohan introduced me to Allan Menagh, the ex-CEO of Kumon, and we hit it off immediately. Allan became an advisor and eventually the Head of Global Partnerships for Success Tutoring. Through him, we expanded the brand internationally. It was through a series of big, bold connections like these that we built the foundation for a truly global organisation.

LESSONS FROM BUILDING A BUSINESS

Starting a business requires big thinking from day one. There's a saying, "Shoot for the moon. Even if you miss, you'll land among the stars." That's the kind of mindset you need. I've always aimed high because I knew that even if I didn't reach every single goal, I'd end up somewhere remarkable.

People often ask me, "Isn't it risky to think big?" I'd argue it's riskier not to. When you aim small, you limit yourself. Success is not about achieving every single goal; it's about pushing your boundaries, learning from the experience, and moving forwards with the knowledge you've gained. Thinking big is a commitment to learning, growing, and always striving for more.

And let me tell you this: most people don't achieve their goals because they aim too low. If you think small, you'll stay small. But when you think big, you open yourself up to greater opportunities and achievements than you ever imagined.

THE TUTORPRENEUR GROWTH PYRAMID: CLIMBING THE LADDER OF SUCCESS

Success in the tutoring business isn't achieved overnight – it's a journey that requires continuous growth and development. The Tutorpreneur Growth Pyramid is a visual framework that illustrates the hierarchy of skills and strategies needed to evolve from a solo tutor to a multi-location franchise owner.

Each layer of the pyramid builds upon the one below, creating a solid foundation for sustainable growth.

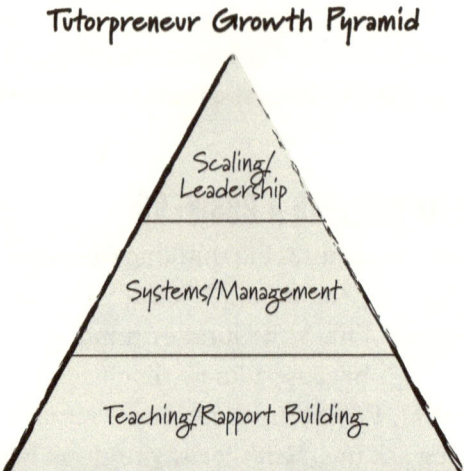

Imagine your journey as a pyramid. At the base are the essential skills every tutor must master. As you move up the pyramid, you develop more advanced operational and leadership capabilities, ultimately reaching the peak where you become a successful franchise leader.

1. Base: Foundational Skills (Teaching & Rapport Building)

The foundation of the pyramid is where every tutorpreneur begins. This layer focuses on mastering the core skills required to provide an exceptional tutoring experience. These include:

- **Teaching Effectiveness:** Understanding how to deliver content in a way that resonates with students.
- **Rapport Building:** Establishing trust and a positive relationship with students to foster engagement and motivation.

Without a strong foundation, it's impossible to build a sustainable business. This stage is crucial for gaining the trust of your initial clients and building your reputation.

2. Middle: Operational Skills
(Systems & Team Management)

Once the foundational skills are in place, the next step is to develop the operational skills necessary to scale your business beyond yourself. This layer focuses on:

- **Systems Implementation:** Creating processes and systems that ensure consistency in service delivery.
- **Team Management:** Hiring, training, and managing a team of tutors to deliver the same high-quality experience you've built your reputation on.

At this stage, you're transitioning from being an individual tutor to a business owner. The goal is to ensure your tutoring business can operate smoothly without your constant involvement.

3. Top: Advanced Strategies
(Scaling & Leadership)

At the top of the pyramid are the advanced strategies required to grow a multi-location franchise and become a true leader in the tutoring industry. This layer includes:

- **Scaling the Business:** Opening additional locations, expanding your offerings, and increasing your impact.
- **Leadership Development:** Becoming a visionary leader who inspires and empowers your team to achieve their best.

This stage is about thinking big. It's where you shift your mindset from managing a business to leading a movement. You're no longer just running a tutoring centre – you're building a brand and creating a legacy.

WHY THE TUTORPRENEUR GROWTH PYRAMID MATTERS

The Tutorpreneur Growth Pyramid provides a roadmap for tutors at every stage of their journey. It shows that success isn't about jumping straight to the top – it's about mastering each layer before moving on to the next. By following this framework, you ensure that your business is built on a solid foundation, ready to scale and thrive.

As the famous saying goes, *"The journey of a thousand miles begins with a single step."* The Tutorpreneur Growth Pyramid reminds us that each step matters, and with the right mindset and strategies, you can climb to the top and achieve lasting success.

THINKING BIG TO CHANGE THE WORLD

The secret sauce to success is simple: think big and work relentlessly towards your vision. That's it. There's no magic wand, no hidden formula. It's about having the courage to dream boldly and the discipline to back those dreams with hard work.

It's my hope that Success Tutoring will continue to grow, evolve, and impact lives globally. But the real success isn't in the number of locations we have or the revenue we generate. It's in the lives we touch and the futures we help shape. That's why I always say, don't think small. Challenge yourself to think bigger than you've ever dared. Set your sights high, work like you mean it, and don't let anything or anyone hold you back.

If you want success, remember this: the secret sauce isn't about finding a shortcut. It's about having the audacity to think big, the grit to work hard, and the resilience to keep going. And when you do, you'll find that there's no limit to what you can achieve.

CHAPTER 15

LOCATION, LOCATION, LOCATION

When it comes to running a successful business, there's one key decision that can make or break your journey from the outset: choosing the right location. I can't stress enough how crucial this is. Whether you're setting up a local café, a retail store, or, as in my case, a tutoring centre, your choice of location becomes the foundation for your success. With Success Tutoring, I quickly learned that where we operate impacts everything from customer traffic to brand perception and, most importantly, the franchise's bottom line.

THE POWER OF A GREAT LOCATION

I've come to realise that a location is more than just a physical address; it's an essential part of a business's identity. For a tutoring centre, we're not looking for high foot traffic the way a café or a retail shop would. Rather, we prioritise factors like ease of access for parents, external signage, and the right kind of visibility. With tutoring, our primary goal is to be a convenient and attractive option for parents who need to drop off and pick up their children without hassle. It's a different kind of visibility we're aiming for.

Consider this: 80% of consumers prefer to shop within a 10-minute drive from home, and tutoring customers are no different. Families want convenience and accessibility. A prime location can reduce friction, making it easier for customers to commit to regular sessions. Plus, signage can be a powerful tool – franchises with visible signage experience a 30% increase in engagement. And in our business, every small advantage helps.

THE CHECKLIST FOR SUCCESS TUTORING LOCATIONS

When evaluating locations, we consider several essential criteria. At Success Tutoring, we aim for spaces between 50 to 150 square metres with easy drop-off points, proximity to local shopping centres, and accessible parking. A good location has the potential to elevate a tutoring centre's status in the community. There's something to be said about having your business located near a trusted shopping centre or a prominent neighbourhood spot – it adds an air of legitimacy.

I remember when I signed the lease for our first official Success Tutoring location. Up until that point, I had been running everything out of my parents' house. Two years into the business, we were ready to expand. The stars aligned, and two prime locations opened up in quick succession. This opportunity, though unexpected, allowed us to establish a strong foothold in the community. Sometimes, the right location finds you when you're ready for it, even before you consciously make the decision to grow.

UNDERSTANDING THE DEMOGRAPHICS

Each area has a unique customer profile, and it's vital to understand this before making any decisions. Demographics play a significant role in shaping the services we offer. For example, in an affluent area, families might prioritise vacation time, meaning attendance fluctuates based on the season. In other neighbourhoods, especially those with a strong emphasis on academics, parents want their children to excel beyond the standard curriculum.

A franchisee needs to know their community. At Success Tutoring, we don't just operate out of one mold; we adapt based on the area's needs. I've always believed that for a business to truly thrive, it must connect with the people it serves on a personal level. Being in tune with the local customer base allows us to adjust our marketing approach and how we communicate our values.

A FEW STORIES FROM THE FIELD

Location has played a pivotal role in the growth of many of our centres. Once, we secured a location that was slightly off the beaten path – a spot in an office building's first floor. There was limited foot traffic, which initially worried some of the franchise partners. However, the visibility from the street due to large, bold signage and ample parking made this spot one of our most successful centres.

There have also been missteps. I once helped a franchise partner secure a location before they signed the agreement, eager to get everything set up. I was excited and saw great potential in the area. Unfortunately, they backed out, and the location ended up becoming a copycat business. That experience taught me a valuable lesson: always secure commitments before diving head-first into location logistics. This approach keeps both sides accountable and saves everyone from unnecessary risks.

BALANCING TRADE-OFFS

There's always a trade-off when choosing a location. Sometimes, we find great spots with high visibility but slightly higher rent. Other times, we secure more affordable spaces with less street traffic. For Success Tutoring, the priority is securing spaces that meet our core needs while staying within budget. We'd rather focus on convenience for the parents over flashy storefronts.

The tutoring industry doesn't require the high visibility that restaurants or retail stores do. Our centres thrive in locations that aren't necessarily prime retail spots, but rather places that are functional, accessible, and well-connected to the community.

BUILDING A RELATIONSHIP WITH LANDLORDS

When selecting a location, I've found that landlords can either become valuable partners or challenging roadblocks. A good relationship with a landlord can ease the leasing process, especially during tough times. For instance, during COVID-19, many businesses had to renegotiate their lease terms to survive. At Success Tutoring, we navigated these challenges by being proactive with our landlords, but that doesn't mean it was easy. In some cases, negotiating lease terms felt like pulling teeth.

This experience underscored the importance of lease agreements with longer terms. Many of our leases are set up for 15 years, providing stability for both parties. A longer lease term means less turnover and more room for growth. It also mitigates the risk of sudden relocations that could disrupt the business and impact our clients.

PRACTICAL TIPS FOR CHOOSING THE RIGHT LOCATION

Over the years, I've come up with a set of "golden rules" for finding the right business location. First, ensure there's access to parking and that it's easy for customers to drop off their kids. Next, look at the neighbourhood and assess the vibe – is it family-friendly? Will parents feel comfortable bringing their children here? Finally, don't rush the process. It's tempting to dive into an exciting new opportunity, but patience is key. The right spot might not be the one with the best price but the one with the most potential for growth and customer retention.

When considering a space, I advise prospective franchise partners to look at the area at different times of the day. Observe traffic patterns, the general safety of the location, and how it feels at night. The right location will stand out in ways that go beyond the numbers.

ADAPTING TO THE TIMES

As more companies embrace remote work, commercial spaces have become more available. This shift presents opportunities for us to explore locations in areas that were once beyond our reach. It also allows us to rethink our space needs. While location is still crucial, flexibility has become an increasingly important consideration.

The COVID-19 pandemic taught us that adaptation is everything. We transitioned to online learning, maintained our customer base, and came out stronger. This experience reminded me that while location is important, resilience and adaptability ultimately make a business successful.

THE FUTURE OF SUCCESS TUTORING LOCATIONS

As we continue to expand, our approach to choosing locations is becoming more refined. We're now working directly with property developers and landlords to find the best spots for new centres. Instead of relying solely on real estate agents, we're forging partnerships that align with our values and ensure a consistent experience across all locations. This strategic move allows us to have more control over the spaces we choose, creating environments that support our mission of motivating, inspiring, and uplifting students.

UNDERSTANDING YOUR COMMUNITY

In the end, the saying "location, location, location" holds true – but it's about more than just where you are. It's about understanding your community, aligning with the needs of your clients, and finding a spot that allows your business to thrive. For Success Tutoring, location is a foundation, but it's also a canvas where we paint our values and shape our brand.

The right location is like a partnership. It's an investment in the future, a commitment to our students and their families, and a reflection of who we are. We're not just finding spaces; we're creating places where children feel motivated, parents feel supported, and communities feel connected. And in doing so, we're building something bigger than just a business – we're building a legacy.

CHAPTER 16

SELLING FRANCHISES LIKE HOTCAKES

When I first set out to grow Success Tutoring, franchising felt like a far-off dream. The image in my mind was clear, though, and I remember spending a night at the office, with the early vision of what this company could be. I opened up Google, found a map of Sydney, and placed the Success Tutoring logo over every area we'd expand into. The map was covered with these logos – a vision of Success Tutoring everywhere. I printed it, hung it up, and could almost hear the whispers in the background. Some of the team laughed; they couldn't imagine the reality I was creating. One joked, "Michael is going to take over the country with Success Tutoring." It was said half in jest, but I could sense a bit of wonder too.

Franchising was never just about selling. It was about offering people the opportunity to invest in something bigger than themselves – an opportunity to help students and improve communities. That's what fuelled me during those early days when I was just starting to market the franchise.

It took me eight long months to sell the very first franchise.

During that time, I tried everything I could think of. I invested thousands of dollars, throwing things at the wall to see what would stick. I put Success Tutoring on franchise directories, created a dedicated franchise website, and ran ads on social media. I didn't stop because, deep down, I knew this idea was valuable. People just needed to see what I saw.

SELLING BY NOT SELLING

If I learned one thing about selling franchises, it's that the conventional approach doesn't work. It's not about hard selling; it's about finding the right people who share the vision and aligning their goals with the franchise's mission. I started thinking less about selling and more about recruiting. I wanted partners, people who believed in the potential of Success Tutoring and would work tirelessly to help students succeed. I learned to be selective. I had to find people I believed in just as much as they believed in the brand.

For example, let me share the story of my first franchise sale. It was to Alex, a former teacher of mine. I remember those days well; I was desperate to get the ball rolling. I met Alex through a networking group from our old school, the "Old Boys Union". When we reconnected, I saw potential in him as a franchise partner. He invited me over for dinner one night. I remember showing up, leaving my laptop in the car, and enjoying a risotto dinner with his family. Afterward, Alex asked me to share what I'd been working on, and I returned to my car to grab the laptop. We moved to another room, and I presented my vision of Success Tutoring. Alex was interested, but I could tell he wanted to know if this was the right decision for his family and their future.

I wasn't selling him on tutoring. I was selling him on the impact he could have and the legacy he could build for his family. When he finally agreed, it was like the floodgates opened. We weren't just a tutoring company anymore; we were a franchise with partners who believed in our mission.

BUILDING INTEREST AND CREATING DEMAND

After Alex, I started building momentum. Each sale became easier, not because I'd changed the product, but because the word was spreading. It turns out, in the franchise world, people talk. They share experiences, they ask questions, and they notice when things work. I learned that thriving franchise locations do the marketing for you. People don't need to hear about your success from an ad; they need to hear about it from someone living it.

But marketing still plays a role, and that's where I started thinking about who Success Tutoring was really for. I initially targeted teachers. It made sense: they understood education and cared deeply about students. However, there was a hurdle – many didn't have the financial resources to invest. I realised we needed to cast a wider net and started targeting anyone over 25 who wanted to make a difference and was ready to invest in a proven system. As the interest grew, so did our vetting process. We needed people who were passionate and would work hard to grow their own locations. And this was a game-changer.

STANDING OUT IN A CROWDED MARKET

As we sold more franchises, people began to ask what made Success Tutoring different. Why were we growing so fast? It's simple: our franchise partners get an exceptional return on their investment. From the start, we adopted a gym-style membership model that gave franchise partners a solid foundation of members from day one. They weren't just opening a centre and hoping for clients to trickle in; they were stepping into a business with momentum. This was something no other tutoring brand was doing.

Our focus is on results, not just for our students, but for the franchise partners. People ask about our unique selling points, and while we have our six pillars – Personalised Program, Exceptional Results, Inspirational Tutors, Motivational Learning, Community Focus, and Flexible Scheduling – the real selling point is that our franchise partners see a tangible return on their investment. We're able to show them real stories of people just like them who changed their lives by joining Success Tutoring.

One example that comes to mind is Sam. He was a teacher who wanted a change, and Success Tutoring gave him the opportunity. He started with just 57 members but grew to over 100 in less than two months. Then there's Fernand, who left his job as an engineer. Today, he's running a successful centre with over 350 weekly members. He doesn't even have to manage it directly anymore; he's hired a team to do that, and now he's exploring other investment opportunities.

LESSONS LEARNED

Over the years, I've refined my approach to selling franchises. My biggest takeaway? You don't sell by selling. Instead, you find out what potential franchise partners are looking for, and you solve that problem for them. Everyone has their own reason for buying a franchise. Some want to leave their 9-to-5 job, others love teaching, and some are simply looking for an exciting new business opportunity. Once you understand their motivation, you can help them see how Success Tutoring aligns with their goals.

I remember one situation vividly. Two potential franchise partners approached me, and we started looking at locations and negotiating leases before they'd signed the agreement. They ended up backing out, and to my surprise, they started a business that was almost an exact replica of Success Tutoring.

This experience taught me a tough but valuable lesson: only move forwards with people who are fully committed, and don't let enthusiasm cloud your judgement.

Patience is crucial in this business. On average, it can take anywhere from one to four months to close a sale. But I'd rather wait and find the right partner than rush the process and end up with someone who isn't aligned with our values. Selling franchises is like a marriage. You have to set clear expectations and understand each other's roles. Transparency, trust, and clear communication are the cornerstones of a strong franchise relationship.

LOOKING FORWARDS

Today, as I look at the expanding network of Success Tutoring locations, I think back to that map with our logos covering Sydney. What was once just an idea has turned into a reality that impacts thousands of students and provides business opportunities for people who are ready to take charge of their own futures. I often say that we're just getting started. The goal is to expand across Earth – and one day, into space.

The lesson I want to leave with you is that when it comes to selling franchises, it's not about the hard sell. Focus on building relationships, understanding your partners, and ensuring you have a product that truly delivers value. When you do that, you won't have to sell at all. The results will speak for themselves.

By focusing on the product, delivering for the customers, and ensuring the franchise network's success, you create a powerful engine that practically sells itself. Thriving, successful locations are the best marketing you could ever ask for. And if you keep working towards your vision with clarity, patience, and purpose, you'll find yourself selling franchises – like hotcakes.

CHAPTER 17

HOW TO RUN A REALLY SUCCESSFUL TUTORING BUSINESS

When I started Success Tutoring, I didn't have a handbook or a guide to follow. I learned a lot from personal experience, from making mistakes, and, most importantly, from the students I had the privilege to tutor. What I can share now comes from years of effort, relentless belief in what I was doing, and countless experiences – both successes and setbacks. If you're looking to start a tutoring business or take yours to the next level, here are some foundational insights and stories from my journey that I hope will inspire and guide you.

FOCUS ON RESULTS FIRST

The most important measure of success in any tutoring business is the results you deliver. This might seem obvious, but you'd be surprised how many tutoring centres fail to prioritise it. I always remind my team that, at the end of the day, parents come to us because they want to see their children thrive academically. If we aren't delivering results, nothing else matters.

When I first started, I didn't have flashy marketing or tons of resources – I had to make miracles happen with what I had. There was Anthony, a student who came to us with a serious lack of confidence in his studies. Through consistent support, he not only saw a significant improvement in his grades but also discovered a passion for pharmaceutical research. Today, he's pursuing a degree in advanced science with plans for a Master's. Stories like Anthony's reinforce why focusing on results is so critical. I remember seeing his mother cry from how proud she was of her son. They remind us that our work has a profound impact on our students' futures.

THE POWER OF MARKETING AND RESOURCES

I learned quickly that marketing in a tutoring business is not about reinventing the wheel but about focusing on what works. Early on, I struggled with getting the right resources for Success Tutoring. It got to the point where I received a copyright infringement notice from a competitor. I had to hire a lawyer to sort it out and ensure we were using materials legally. The lesson here is to build and develop your own resources over time, rather than relying on others.

Once you've created resources, you need to keep them updated. Quality resources are essential, but don't let that hold you back from starting. In the beginning, we were often making resources right before the lesson started! It was stressful, to say the least, but it taught me a lot about resourcefulness and resilience.

UNDERSTANDING THE RIGHT BUSINESS MODEL

For Success Tutoring, I chose a gym membership–style model. There's a reason for this. I've tried almost every model out there: one-on-one tutoring, group sessions, and even online tutoring. Nothing struck the balance between student convenience, tutor consistency, and franchisee profitability like the membership model did.

This model also transformed how we approach scheduling and payments. Students have the flexibility to attend classes without being locked into a term-based schedule. For tutors, this means a more predictable schedule with hours in blocks, not scattered one-off sessions. And for franchise partners, this translates to a more consistent revenue stream, even during school holidays.

BUILDING A SOLID TEAM

Your tutors are the face of your business, and the quality of your service will only be as good as the people you hire. The biggest lesson I learned about hiring came when I found out I'd employed someone with a questionable background – a lawyer who had previously been found guilty of drug-related charges. This was a wake-up call. I made it a rule that background checks and police clearances would be non-negotiable for every hire moving forwards.

In the early days, it's easy to hire friends or people you know. But I realised that professionalism and competence should always come first. It's about finding people who share your values, who can uphold the standards you set, and who will work with you to deliver exceptional results for students.

OPERATIONS THAT SCALE

There's a saying I live by: "What got you here, won't get you there." If you're serious about scaling, you'll need systems that can handle it. In the beginning, running the business on spreadsheets and Google Docs worked fine. But as we grew, I had to implement more advanced systems for scheduling, tracking progress, and managing client relationships. This infrastructure allowed us to expand beyond one location and scale to multiple centres across the country.

One of the most valuable lessons I've learned is that as you scale, the requirements for staff, structure, and systems grow with you. It's crucial to have scalable operations in place so that you can focus on growth rather than being stuck in the day-to-day management of each location.

THE IMPORTANCE OF WORD-OF-MOUTH

I'm a firm believer in the power of word-of-mouth marketing. You could spend thousands of dollars on ads, but nothing beats a parent telling another parent how their child went from failing to excelling because of your services. Once we reach about 50 members at a location, we see a strong word-of-mouth effect kick in, and new sign-ups happen almost organically. Happy customers will always be your best marketers.

I remember one particular success story that led to a cascade of referrals. A student named Ishika had started with us struggling academically but went on to achieve an ATAR that earned her a scholarship. She became one of our tutors, and later, at the age of 23, opened her own Success Tutoring franchise. That's what real results do – they build credibility and drive sustainable growth.

RETAINING STUDENTS FOR THE LONG HAUL

Customer retention is essential. Acquiring new customers is always more costly than keeping the ones you have. Retained students and satisfied parents become brand ambassadors. The secret to retention lies in balancing the relationships you have with customers and the value you provide. When families trust you and feel valued, they stick around.

The membership model has been especially helpful for retention, as it offers flexibility and makes our services feel more accessible. By constantly providing value and fostering a community feel within the centres, we've been able to build strong relationships with our students and their families.

NAVIGATING CHALLENGES

In the early days, I ran Success Tutoring on a one-on-one tutoring model. It seemed like a good idea at the time, but it nearly bankrupted the business. We were dependent on tutor availability, and if a student didn't show up, we wouldn't get paid. The administrative burden was heavy, and the income was inconsistent. Switching to group tutoring and a membership model saved us, allowing us to balance scheduling, reduce costs, and boost profit margins.

The transition was tough, but looking back, it was the best decision I could have made. It taught me that flexibility is vital. You have to be willing to adapt, to pivot, and to trust that the changes you're making will bring you closer to success.

IF YOU'RE PASSIONATE, TAKE THE LEAP

If you're passionate about tutoring, just go for it! You won't know unless you try. There are so many rewarding moments in this business. I still remember the early days when I'd take cash from tutoring sessions and deposit it every Monday. I loved seeing that amount grow each week – it was a tangible sign of the progress we were making.

And I remember racing against time to create resources before classes, and that intense thrill of making it all work under pressure. It wasn't easy, but it was worth every moment. Passion and a relentless drive to make a difference are what will sustain you through the long nights and early mornings.

FOCUS ON GROWTH – USE THE FRANCHISE FLYWHEEL APPROACH

Decide on your path and go for it. To run a very successful business you must have the end in mind. One way to think of having the end in mind, is by using the Flywheel approach. When you think of a flywheel, imagine a heavy wheel that takes significant effort to start spinning. At first, it feels almost impossible to get it moving. You push and push, and it inches forwards. But as you keep pushing consistently, momentum builds, and soon, the flywheel is spinning with ease. The same principle applies to growing a business. I call it the *Franchise Flywheel*.

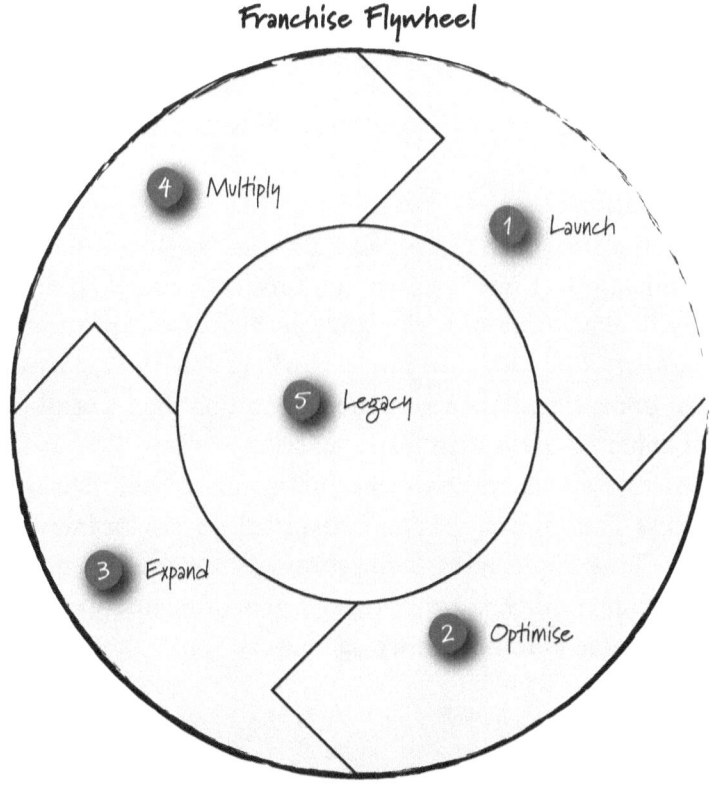

The Franchise Flywheel consists of five key stages that create a self-sustaining cycle of success. Each stage builds upon the previous one, ensuring that growth is continuous and scalable. Let's break down each stage:

1. Launch

Every franchise begins with a launch. This is the stage where new franchise partners enter the network, armed with the tools, training, and support provided by Success Tutoring. The launch phase is critical because it sets the foundation for future success. A well-executed launch ensures that franchise partners hit the ground running and start building momentum from day one.

During this phase, franchise partners are focused on setting up their centres, learning the systems, and starting to acquire their first students. Success Tutoring provides a step-by-step roadmap to make this process as smooth as possible.

2. Optimise

Once the franchise is up and running, the focus shifts to optimisation. This involves refining operations, improving efficiency, and ensuring that all processes are running smoothly. The optimise phase is where franchise partners learn to maximise their revenue, streamline their workflows, and enhance the student experience.

At this stage, franchise partners work closely with the Success Tutoring support team to identify areas for improvement. This might include fine-tuning marketing strategies, enhancing tutor training programs, or implementing new technologies to improve service delivery.

3. Expand

With a solid foundation and optimised operations, franchise partners are ready to expand. Expansion can mean growing the number of students served, offering additional services, or even opening additional locations. The key to this phase is scaling without losing the quality and consistency that Success Tutoring is known for.

The expansion phase is where franchise partnerss begin to see significant returns on their initial investment. By leveraging the proven systems and brand reputation of Success Tutoring, they can confidently grow their businesses and increase their impact.

4. Multiply

The multiply phase takes expansion to the next level. At this stage, franchise partners become mentors and leaders within the Success Tutoring network. They may take on roles in supporting new franchise partners, sharing best practices, and contributing to the overall growth of the brand.

Multiplication isn't just about opening more centres; it's about creating a ripple effect of success throughout the entire network. Franchise partners who reach this phase play a critical role in sustaining the momentum of the Franchise Flywheel.

5. Legacy

The final stage of the Franchise Flywheel is legacy. This is where franchise partners have built something that lasts beyond their direct involvement. It's about creating a lasting impact in their communities, contributing to the education sector, and leaving a mark on the Success Tutoring brand.

Legacy is about more than just financial success – it's about changing lives. Franchise partners who reach this stage have built a business that continues to thrive, empowering students and families for years to come. Their influence extends beyond the walls of their centres, shaping the future of education.

THE FUTURE IS FULL OF POSSIBILITIES

As I look to the future, I can see how technology will continue to reshape tutoring. Artificial intelligence is definitely a part of that future. It will allow us to provide even more personalised learning experiences and reach students in new and innovative ways.

The journey of running a successful tutoring business is not a straightforward path, but it's one filled with purpose and impact. If you're ready to make a difference in students' lives, to put in the work, and to grow something that lasts, then you're on the right track. Remember, success is about more than profits. It's about knowing that what you're doing matters, that you're making a lasting impact, and that you're building something bigger than yourself.

A FAMILY'S JOURNEY: BUILDING A THRIVING TUTORING BUSINESS TOGETHER

Sandra & Brendan, Success Tutoring North Lakes, QLD

Launching a business is never a small decision, but for us, it was about more than just starting a new venture – it was about building a family legacy. As a husband-and-wife team, we wanted to create something that would not only bring us financial freedom but also allow us to make a positive impact on our community. When we discovered Success Tutoring, we knew it was the perfect fit.

From the very beginning, we were committed to running a really successful tutoring business, and Success Tutoring gave us the roadmap to do just that. The systems, processes, and training through SuccessAcademy were instrumental in helping us launch with confidence. We didn't have to guess our way through starting a business – the blueprint was already there. All we had to do was follow it.

When we opened Success Tutoring North Lakes, we were thrilled to welcome over 70 foundation members from day one. This immediate success wasn't luck – it was the result of following a proven business model. We focused on building strong relationships with students and parents, creating a welcoming and supportive environment, and ensuring that every student felt motivated, inspired, and uplifted.

Running a successful tutoring business is about more than just academics. It's about understanding your community's needs, building trust, and delivering a service that genuinely changes lives. We've seen firsthand how our approach has transformed students – not just in their grades but in their confidence and self-belief. Parents are grateful, students are thriving, and our business continues to grow steadily.

Working together as a couple has also been one of the most rewarding aspects of this journey. We each bring different strengths to the table – Sandra focuses on the day-to-day operations and student engagement, while

Brendan handles marketing, strategy, and community outreach. This division of roles allows us to manage the business efficiently and maintain a healthy work-life balance.

One of the key lessons we've learned is that consistency is key. Success doesn't happen overnight, but when you follow the systems in place and stay committed to delivering exceptional service, the results speak for themselves. We've built a thriving business by focusing on student outcomes, strong relationships, and operational excellence.

For anyone looking to run a successful tutoring business, our advice is simple: follow the systems, stay focused on your community, and trust the process. The Success Tutoring model works because it's built on proven principles. If you're willing to put in the effort and genuinely care about your students' success, you'll build a business that not only changes your life but also transforms the lives of those around you.

Today, we're proud to say that we've built more than just a tutoring centre – we've built a community of learners. Our journey with Success Tutoring has been life-changing, and we're excited to continue growing, making an impact, and inspiring the next generation of students.

CHAPTER 18

BUYING A FRANCHISE CAN CHANGE YOUR LIFE

When most people think of franchise ownership, they picture a turnkey business – a ready-made machine designed to print money, so they can simply plug in and profit. But the reality of franchise ownership is far more profound. It's not just about the immediate returns; it's about the opportunity to transform your entire life. It's a path that can lead you away from a mundane 9-to-5 job, towards the freedom and fulfilment that come with owning a business. If you're truly dedicated, buying the right franchise can be the gateway to living a life filled with purpose, passion, and potential.

THE POWER OF FRANCHISING: MORE THAN A BUSINESS MODEL

Franchising isn't just a way to expand a brand; it's a powerful mechanism that enables the people who invest in it to thrive. As a business model, it provides a tremendous advantage by allowing franchise partners to learn from each other and the franchisor. In our Success Tutoring network, I see this all the time. One of our franchise partners, for instance, came up with a brilliant idea for a school holiday program called "Mind Painters". It quickly became a hit and inspired other franchise partners to create and run similar programs. This collaborative environment is one of the best aspects of owning a franchise. You're not just operating in isolation; you're part of a larger ecosystem where innovation and ideas flow freely.

Take that first step and choose a franchise you believe in. The benefits of the right franchise extend far beyond an established brand and proven business model. Yes, those are essential, but the real value is in the support network and the collective wisdom you gain. Every franchisee is part of a greater whole, learning from each other's experiences and helping each other grow.

THE TRANSFORMATIVE POWER OF OWNING A FRANCHISE

The most fulfilling part of franchising, for me, is seeing the transformation it brings to our franchise partners' lives. There's Sam, a former full-time teacher who started with 57 students and quickly grew his Success Tutoring location to over 100 students within a few months. For him, Success Tutoring wasn't just a business; it was a chance to redefine his career. He went from being overworked and underpaid to thriving in a business he could be passionate about, impacting young lives and reaping financial rewards.

And then there's Fernand, a former engineer who took a leap of faith to open a franchise location. Today, he has more than 350 weekly members, a full-time manager, and he's become an investor. Fernand's life changed so profoundly that he now lives in a penthouse overlooking Darling Harbour. I've seen it myself, and the view is magnificent. But even more powerful than the view is the freedom and sense of achievement he's earned through his dedication. Buying a franchise didn't just change his bank account; it changed his entire outlook on life.

FRANCHISE OWNERSHIP: THE REALITY AND THE MISCONCEPTIONS

Now, I'd be remiss if I didn't address the misconceptions surrounding franchising. There's this idea that buying a franchise is like purchasing a money printer: put cash in, and watch cash come out. If only it were that simple! While a franchise offers an established business model, it still requires commitment, hard work, and often, significant capital. Franchise owners can delegate tasks, but they're the ones who have to set up those systems first. You're still building a business – one that needs your energy, dedication, and leadership.

Of course, there's another misconception that the franchise model is completely foolproof. Nothing in business is ever guaranteed. A franchise can offer a road map, but you're the one who has to follow it. A franchise model provides a significant advantage, yes, but it doesn't absolve you from the responsibility of steering your own ship.

Consider the story of Blockbuster, for example. Blockbuster was once a titan in the video rental industry. It had a massive franchise network and an instantly recognisable brand, but failed to adapt to the rise of streaming technology. As the industry evolved, the company stagnated, dragging franchise partners down with it. The takeaway? Make sure your franchise partner is forward-thinking and willing to change with the times.

FAMILY FORCE FRAMEWORK: BUILDING A LEGACY THROUGH A FAMILY-DRIVEN BUSINESS

The path to financial freedom doesn't have to be travelled alone. The Family Force Framework is a strategic, phased approach that empowers families – particularly dual-income households – to transition from corporate jobs to full-time entrepreneurship through a tutoring franchise. By working together, families can build a scalable business that achieves financial independence and leaves a lasting legacy for future generations.

This framework emphasises the power of family collaboration, with each partner playing a vital role in the business's growth. Here's how it works:

Phase 1: Planting the Foundation
Objective: Establish the first tutoring franchise as a family-run venture.

In this initial phase, the wife leaves her part-time job to launch the business, while the husband continues working full-time to provide financial stability. The focus is on building a strong foundation for the first tutoring centre.

Steps:
- **Wife Takes the Lead:** Completes SuccessAcademy training and manages daily operations.
- **Husband Supports Strategically:** Assists with planning, marketing, and administrative tasks during evenings and weekends.
- **Launch with Purpose:** Create a welcoming, community-focused environment to attract students and families.

Why This Works: The husband's income reduces financial pressure, allowing the wife to focus on growth. By bringing hands-on leadership, the wife can build meaningful relationships with students and parents, establishing trust and loyalty.

Milestone: The first tutoring centre becomes operational, covering costs and generating consistent revenue.

Phase 2: Scaling with Confidence
Objective: Expand operations by launching a second location.
Once the first site is stable, the family begins planning for expansion. The husband transitions into the business part-time, focusing on strategic growth.

Steps:
- **Optimise the First Site:** Hire a centre manager to handle daily operations and refine systems.
- **Begin Expansion Planning:** Use profits from the first centre to invest in a second location.
- **Husband Gets Involved:** Supports financial management, marketing, and the overall expansion strategy.

Why This Works: The wife ensures stability at the first centre while the husband brings his corporate experience to scale the business. Expanding with a proven model minimises risk and builds momentum.

Milestone: The second site launches successfully, with the husband ready to transition into the business full-time.

Phase 3: Achieving Freedom Together
Objective: Create a fully family-operated enterprise with multiple thriving locations.
The final phase sees both partners fully immersed in the business, focusing on long-term growth and legacy-building.

Steps:
- **Husband Quits Corporate:** Transitions into the business full-time to oversee high-level strategy.
- **Focus on Growth:** Explore new revenue streams such as online tutoring, workshops, or additional franchises.
- **Strengthen the Family Legacy:** Mentor children or younger family members in the business and reinvest profits for future growth.

Why This Works: With both partners fully dedicated, the business benefits from a unified vision and shared goals. Financial freedom allows the family to prioritise flexibility and work-life balance, creating a sustainable and impactful enterprise.

Milestone: The business generates enough income to replace both partners' corporate salaries, achieving financial independence for the family.

KEY BENEFITS OF THE FAMILY FORCE FRAMEWORK
- **Minimised Risk:** The husband's full-time income provides stability, reducing financial stress.
- **Balanced Transition:** The wife leads initially, and the husband joins once the business is ready for full-time growth.
- **Shared Responsibility:** Each family member plays a specific role, leveraging their strengths for collective success.
- **Scalable Model:** The phased approach creates a replicable system for opening multiple locations without becoming overburdened.

THE FAMILY FORCE MANIFESTO
- We trust each other to build something bigger than ourselves.
- Our business is a family legacy, not just an income source.
- We support each other's strengths and divide responsibilities for success.
- Together, we create a life of freedom, flexibility, and purpose.

The Family Force Framework transforms the dream of entrepreneurship into a practical, achievable reality for families. It's not just about financial freedom – it's about building a legacy that impacts future generations.

Making the Leap: What You Need to Know Before Buying a Franchise

If you're considering buying a franchise, start by doing your homework. One of the greatest aspects of a franchise model is that you're not in this alone. But that doesn't mean you should jump in blindly. Many franchise agreements last five or more years, which means you're committing to a long-term partnership. Make sure it's the right fit for you. Research the industry, talk to current franchise owners, and make sure you align with the franchise's vision and values.

A key question to ask yourself is whether you're prepared to embrace change. Buying a franchise can – and often will – transform not just your work life but your entire lifestyle. Think of your family and loved ones, too. This isn't just a personal venture; it's one that can affect the people closest to you. The flexibility of running your own business can give you more time with family, but it will also require sacrifices, especially in the beginning. Be ready for both.

The Right Franchise Can Change Your Life

The right franchise isn't a magic bullet, but it can be a life-changing opportunity. When I think of the people who have joined Success Tutoring, I'm constantly amazed by how far they've come. They're building businesses that they're proud of, impacting their communities, and creating futures filled with possibilities. For many, the franchise model was exactly what they needed to transition from a life of monotony to one filled with purpose and passion.

Buying a franchise is like buying a dream with a blueprint attached. It's up to you to bring it to life. The reality is that too many people are unhappy in their 9-to-5 jobs, doing work that drains them instead of inspiring them. But it doesn't have to be that way. You can make the decision to change your life, to pursue something meaningful, and to do so with the support and guidance of a proven system. Don't let fear of the unknown hold you back. Step out with courage, and you may find that owning a franchise is the key to the life you've always wanted.

ENGINEERING A NEW FUTURE: FROM CORPORATE JOB TO BUSINESS OWNER

Fernand, Success Tutoring
Wentworthville, NSW

I never imagined that I would transition from working in one of Australia's largest property development firms to running my own business. For years, I followed the traditional path – go to university, get a stable job, and work your way up the corporate ladder. I completed a Bachelor of Engineering at the University of NSW and landed a position at a major firm, even working in iconic locations like Barangaroo. On paper, it all looked perfect. But deep down, I knew something was missing.

I wanted more. More autonomy, more purpose, and more time to focus on what truly matters to me – family and community. That's when I discovered Success Tutoring and the opportunity to build something of my own.

When I launched Success Tutoring Wentworthville, I wasn't stepping into the unknown. I had a clear roadmap, thanks to the franchise's proven systems and support network. What surprised me most was how quickly I was able to build a team and create a positive impact in my community. Today, I lead a team of dedicated tutors and managers, and we're helping students achieve academic success while inspiring them to reach their full potential.

What I love most about this journey is seeing how tutoring isn't just about grades – it's about changing lives. It's about helping students build confidence, resilience, and a love for learning.

I won't lie – transitioning from a corporate job to business ownership had its challenges. But every step of the way, I felt supported by the Success Tutoring community. I've gone from working for someone else's vision to building my own. And that's the most empowering change of all.

I no longer feel like a cog in a machine. I feel like I'm building a legacy, not just for myself but for my family and my community. Success Tutoring has given me the opportunity to combine my analytical skills with my passion for making a difference. And it's a decision I would make again in a heartbeat.

> If you're thinking about taking the leap into business ownership, here's my advice: have the courage to back yourself. The rewards go far beyond financial success – they're about freedom, impact, and fulfilment.

PART 4

INDUSTRY INSIGHTS

CHAPTER 19

WHAT THE GOVERNMENT WILL NOT TELL YOU

As we dive into this chapter, I want to challenge your perception of the world around you. We live in a society where the government plays a huge role in how we see our lives, careers, and futures. Most people grow up trusting that the systems in place – especially those surrounding education, work, and finances – are designed to help us succeed. But the truth is, the government often keeps key information from us. If you rely solely on the government for guidance, you'll never break free from the rat race or the limits imposed on your potential.

The government has one agenda – staying in power. Politicians are not motivated by helping you achieve your dreams or ensuring your financial freedom. They are driven by re-election. To stay in power, they must secure funding from powerful lobby groups and convince people to vote them in. It's the same cycle every time. But here's what they won't tell you: the real power lies with the ultra-rich, the corporate lobbyists, and big business. They pull the strings. Politicians? They're just players on the stage, performing their roles.

MICHAEL BLACK

THE SCHOOL SYSTEM – A FACTORY FOR WORKERS, NOT THINKERS

One of the most damaging things the government keeps hidden is how the school system is designed to produce workers, not thinkers. From a young age, children are taught to follow a set structure, a curriculum designed to standardise learning and destroy creativity. The system discourages independent thought and focuses on churning out students who will fit into the 9-to-5 mold.

When I was a student, I remember how often I saw this. I'd watch as students' creativity was stifled. Instead of encouraging students to dream big, think differently, or follow their passions, schools pushed us towards one goal: get a job. A "safe" job. That's the government's agenda. If every student became a business owner or entrepreneur, who would fill the corporate offices? Who would work in the factories? They don't want too many business owners because then there would be a shortage of workers.

The school system is like a factory. Every student is treated the same. Individual dreams? Those get left at the door. Creativity? Stamped out. This system is not about helping children reach their potential. It's about programming them to be compliant workers.

If you're a parent reading this, I encourage you to question what's being taught to your children. Homeschooling, while challenging, puts the control of education back into your hands. The government doesn't want more people homeschooling because that means less control for them. It's easier for them to mold children into future workers if parents aren't as involved.

WHY THE GOVERNMENT WANTS YOU IN A JOB

The government is perfectly content with the idea of families working two jobs, with parents having less and less time for their children. Why? Because when parents are busy, the government and school system step in to shape young minds. Teachers, who often have more influence on children than parents, begin to instill beliefs, many of which can limit children's potential.

Now, don't get me wrong – there are fantastic teachers out there. But there's a reason the government underpays teachers. They don't want the brightest minds educating the next generation. They want doers, not thinkers. The teachers who shape the future are often constrained by the same system that prevents true education from flourishing. And many parents don't realise that the influence of teachers can often surpass their own. I remember when I was in primary school, a teacher called the entire class "pigs". When I got home, I told my mum, "I'm a pig!" That's the power of a teacher's influence on a young child.

Teachers sometimes even impose limiting beliefs on students. I remember a moment from year ten when I told a teacher that I wanted a woman who feared God and was a virgin. His response? "In your dreams, you'll never find someone like that these days." This kind of thinking limits our potential. As parents and future business owners, you must guard your children against these limiting beliefs. You must be the protector of their dreams.

THE GOVERNMENT AND BUSINESS – WHAT THEY WON'T TEACH YOU

Let's talk about business. The school system doesn't teach you how to build a business. I studied business in school, and yet I wasn't taught what it really takes to start or run a successful business. The government doesn't want everyone starting businesses because they need employees to keep the economy moving. They need people to pay taxes, and the more employees there are, the more taxes they can collect. In fact, about 50% of tax revenue comes from individuals, while only 25% comes from businesses.

Starting your own business is one of the best ways to reduce your tax burden. As a business owner, you can buy things through the company – like a car used for business, business trips, or office supplies – that help reduce your taxable income. Yet the government doesn't advertise this. Why? Because they need employees. They need people to keep the current system running smoothly.

CREATING A COMPANY – THE GOVERNMENT'S BIGGEST HACK FOR TAXES

One of the easiest ways to reduce taxes is by creating a company. When you own a business, you pay less tax because you can deduct business expenses. Compare this to a regular job, where taxes are automatically deducted from your paycheck at the highest rates.

Most people don't realise this, but creating a company (and eventually, a trust) is one of the smartest financial moves you can make. The government knows this, but they won't tell you because they rely on individual tax revenue to keep the economy going.

THE EDUCATION SYSTEM – WHAT THEY DON'T WANT YOU TO KNOW

I believe, after all my years of research, that children can complete their education from grades K-12 in half the time. That's right – half the time! Six years of schooling is a waste of life. Yet, the government wants children in school for 12 years.

Why? Because the longer they're in school, the more time the government has to program them into workers. They're not interested in educating children to become entrepreneurs or independent thinkers.

Imagine if schools grouped children by ability rather than age. In most schools, kids are held back by their peers simply because they're all the same age. Age becomes a limitation rather than a way to group students based on their skills and talents. Most disability schools already group students by ability. Why isn't this the norm across all schools?

SUCCESS IS IN YOUR HANDS

The bottom line is this: you can't rely on the government for your success. It's up to you. You need to take control of your life, your business, and your future. Don't let the government dictate what you can and cannot do. They won't tell you how to build a business, how to reduce your taxes, or how to live a life of financial freedom. It's not in their interest.

If you're reading this, you already know that you need to break free from the system. The 9-to-5 grind isn't going to bring you financial freedom or happiness. Starting your own business will. When I signed my first commercial lease at 20, I didn't wait for permission from anyone. I knew that I had to learn by doing, by failing, and by succeeding on my own terms. And I did.

YOU HAVE THE POWER

Here's what I want you to do – wake up to the world around you. Realise that the government's system is designed to keep you in a box. But you have the power to break free. Start that business. Take control of your finances. Teach your children how to think, not just what to think. Follow your passion, and don't let anyone – including the government – stand in your way.

Step out of the matrix, take control, and start building your own success. The government won't do it for you. But you, with the right mindset and a plan, can.

CHAPTER 20

THE BROKEN EDUCATION SYSTEM – TUTORING IS NOT THE SOLUTION

Growing up, we were all handed a script. We were told to go to school, study hard, get good grades, and one day, all of it would pay off. We'd land that dream job, climb the ladder, and live happily ever after in a secure, 9-to-5 world. But here's the thing: the education system wasn't designed to cultivate dreamers, creators, or entrepreneurs. It was designed to mold workers.

The entire system we know today was built with that intention. It was shaped by people like John D Rockefeller, a man who once famously said, "I don't want a nation of thinkers, I want a nation of workers." Rockefeller was one of the wealthiest men in history, but his legacy within our educational model is often overlooked. When I dug deeper into the origins of our schooling system, I realised just how meticulously it was engineered to produce not free-thinkers, but people who would slot neatly into a workforce, follow instructions, and serve a machine that churns 9-to-5ers for a living.

Now, let's look at the reality of the classroom. Kids are grouped by age, not by ability. They're required to study subjects that may not align with their strengths or interests, and they're evaluated on an outdated grading scale. And if they struggle? Well, they're often left behind. It's no wonder I receive constant complaints from parents, frustrated and disillusioned with the lack of personalised attention their children receive in school.

A SYSTEM STUCK IN TIME

There's a pervasive issue that's grown larger over time: the school system is fundamentally broken. I've seen it firsthand through years of tutoring, where I'm reminded daily of the limitations students face in traditional schooling. The more I work with these kids, the more I see their true potential. I believe that a student's primary and secondary education could be completed in half the time, if only we removed the unnecessary delays and distractions. I know it's a bold statement, but time and again, I see students come to Success Tutoring, and within weeks, they make remarkable progress.

Consider this: how many times have you asked your child what they learned in school today, only to be met with a blank stare? Or worse, to hear that they were just trying to "get through the day". When I ask parents what they think about their child's education, I often get the same answers – they're unimpressed, frustrated, and at a loss. They're wondering why so much time is being wasted. And I don't blame them.

The biggest robbery happening today is that of time. Children's time is being wasted at an alarming rate. Our current system doesn't encourage kids to find their passions or develop their unique strengths. Instead, it categorises them, shuffles them through standardised tests, and pushes them along a conveyor belt that leads to a cookie-cutter version of success that not everyone is suited for. I was one of those kids who felt this way, too. I couldn't wait to leave school, eager to escape a system that never felt aligned with who I was or what I wanted to become.

THE LIMITS OF TUTORING

As much as I believe in the power of tutoring, I know that it's not the ultimate solution to fix this broken system. Tutoring helps students navigate the system, and it can often give them the support and skills they're missing out on at school. But let's be clear: tutoring isn't here to replace education. The issues within our education system are too ingrained, too systemic, for tutoring alone to fix.

Instead, tutoring acts as a Band-Aid. It addresses some of the symptoms but cannot repair the root of the problem. Tutoring helps students get back on track academically, but it doesn't transform a system that's built to suppress creativity, conformity, and critical thinking. Tutoring doesn't dismantle the fact that students are primarily being trained to memorise and regurgitate information.

I've seen it all too often. A bright student struggles in school not because they lack intelligence, but because the system doesn't cater to their unique learning style. They may fall behind in maths or English because they can't keep up with a teacher who's juggling the needs of 30 other students. And so, the parents seek out tutoring. We help that student, and they begin to make progress, but the same issues persist at school. Tutoring should never have to replace education, but right now, it's doing just that for too many students.

MICHAEL BLACK

A SYSTEM THAT TEACHES OBEDIENCE, NOT INDEPENDENCE

In the traditional school system, students are taught to follow rules, sit quietly, and absorb information. The problem with this is that they're not really being prepared for life. They're being trained for a routine existence, where they'll be encouraged to find a job, stick with it, and never question the path they're on. Think about it: students spend years learning things that may never have any relevance to their lives. Why should a future artist or writer struggle through trigonometry? Why are students required to memorise facts that are only a Google search away?

We need schools that cultivate thinking, that develop problem-solving, that encourage students to explore and pursue their interests. But instead, we see children forced to sit through subjects they're uninterested in, just to pass an exam that has little bearing on their future. What if we flipped the script? Imagine a school system that emphasises real-life skills, emotional intelligence, financial literacy, and the pursuit of passions.

Here's something that has always fascinated me: I once spoke to a teacher who worked with students with disabilities. The school didn't group these children by age; instead, they grouped them by their abilities. I found that absolutely revolutionary. I thought, "Why isn't this model being used everywhere?" If students were placed in classrooms based on ability, rather than age, they could progress at their own pace. It would break down the barriers that hold so many students back, giving them the opportunity to thrive in an environment that truly suits their learning needs.

TEACHERS – OVERWORKED AND UNDERAPPRECIATED

Let's not forget the role of teachers in all of this. I believe that most teachers start out with a passion for educating and a desire to make a difference. But as the years go by, that passion is often dulled by a mountain of administrative tasks, lack of support, and a curriculum that doesn't allow room for creativity. Many teachers are so burdened by paperwork and systemic constraints that they don't have time to actually teach. I've met teachers who are just as disillusioned with the system as the students are, and who can blame them?

Teachers are expected to be everything: educators, counsellors, disciplinarians, and mentors, all while handling excessive class sizes and dealing with parents who are, understandably, frustrated. They're given a curriculum that's more concerned with meeting governmental standards than with fostering genuine learning. No wonder so many of them leave the profession within their first five years. The education system is broken for students, but it's also broken for the teachers who dedicate their lives to it.

THE REALITY OF SCHOOL REPORTS

Another glaring issue is the school reporting system. Often, parents are given reports full of jargon and vague assessments that don't actually tell them much about their child's progress. In primary schools, especially, it's not uncommon for reports to feel more like a checklist than a genuine reflection of a student's achievements and areas for improvement. Parents come to me all the time, baffled by these reports, wondering if their child is truly learning or just going through the motions.

I've seen so many instances where a child's true abilities are overlooked or undervalued. For example, we might perform a diagnostic assessment on a new student at Success Tutoring and find that their academic level is far below what their school reports suggested. It's disheartening to realise that the reports parents rely on are sometimes misleading, leaving gaps that only come to light when we start working with the student one-on-one.

TUTORING: A BAND-AID, NOT A CURE

So, where does tutoring fit into all of this? As much as I believe in the work we do at Success Tutoring, I know that tutoring isn't a long-term solution to the problems within the school system. Tutoring fills the gaps, yes, and it gives students the support they often can't get in a classroom of 30. But it doesn't change the fact that the system itself is fundamentally flawed.

I like to think of tutoring as a safety net. It's there for students who need extra help, who struggle to keep up, or who want to excel beyond the limitations of their regular schoolwork. But it doesn't have the power to restructure the system that put them in that position to begin with. If anything, tutoring has become necessary because of these systemic issues. We are helping students get through the system, but we're not in a position to overhaul it.

REAL SOLUTIONS REQUIRE RADICAL CHANGE

If we're going to truly address the failures of our education system, we need more than tutoring. We need a revolution in the way we think about education. Imagine a system that grouped students by ability, not by age, where they could progress at their own pace, without the pressure of keeping up with peers who may be on a completely different level. Picture classrooms that prioritise project-based learning, encouraging students to work on real-world problems, rather than memorising facts for an exam.

We need to consider alternatives like homeschooling, ability-based learning, and even entire schools dedicated to experiential learning. We need to ask ourselves if it's time to make sweeping changes that align education with the needs of our world today. Why not build a system that encourages students to develop skills they're passionate about, that fosters creativity, and that prepares them for a world where innovation and adaptability are more important than test scores?

DEVELOPING SELF-LEARNING AND CRITICAL THINKING SKILLS

One of the most important skills any student can develop is the ability to think critically and learn independently. In a world where information is at our fingertips, memorisation has taken a back seat to the skill of knowing how to ask the right questions, how to evaluate sources, and how to pursue knowledge that goes beyond the classroom. When I think about the students at Success Tutoring, I don't just want them to succeed academically. I want them to walk away with a lifelong passion for learning, a confidence in their ability to take control of their education.

Thankfully, we live in an age where resources for self-learning are abundant. Students today have access to books, podcasts, and online courses that cover every topic imaginable. They have the opportunity to explore subjects they're curious about, to find their own answers, and to cultivate a love of learning that no traditional classroom can instill. And as parents, mentors, and educators, it's our role to guide them, to encourage them, and to help them find their unique path in a world that desperately needs independent thinkers.

FINAL THOUGHTS: THE CHOICE IS YOURS

The reality is, the school system is what it is. Until a leader steps forwards to demand real change, the system will continue to churn out workers instead of thinkers. And as parents, you have a choice. You can go along with it, or you can take a more active role in your child's education. Recognise that school is not the be-all and end-all. If your child isn't thriving in school, it doesn't mean they won't succeed in life.

I'm personally so convinced of the system's flaws that I know I'll homeschool my own children one day. I want to give them an education that values their time, respects their individuality, and cultivates their unique talents. Because at the end of the day, the greatest gift we can give our children is not a report card filled with good grades, but the confidence to pursue their dreams, the skills to navigate the world, and the knowledge that they have the power to shape their own futures.

PART 4

EXPERT ADVICE

CHAPTER 21

TIPS FOR PARENTS

As parents, you are your child's first teachers, role models, and guides. Your influence on their growth, perspective, and success in life is profound. It's a role of immense responsibility and an incredible opportunity. The tips I'm about to share come from years of working closely with young people and from the lessons I've learned both as a business owner and as someone who deeply values the power of a supportive family.

In today's world, parenting isn't just about providing food, clothing, and shelter; it's about nurturing character, teaching values, and inspiring your children to reach their full potential. Let's dive into these tips, keeping in mind that parenting is as much about guiding and listening as it is about teaching.

1. Stop Having Blind Faith in the School System
One of the biggest mistakes I see parents make is having absolute trust in the school system. Too many times, I've seen reports from schools that don't align with a child's actual

progress or potential. I hear from parents all the time about how their child's school report doesn't reflect the reality they see at home or in tutoring sessions. You have to question things and think independently.

The school system is flawed, and it's not built to bring out the best in every child. The unfortunate reality is that the system can't keep up, and not every teacher has the resources or time to give each student the attention they need. Remember, as parents, you know your child better than anyone else. Be their advocate. Don't take every school report or evaluation as gospel truth. Engage in discussions with teachers, observe your child's progress yourself, and make decisions that align with your understanding of your child's needs.

2. Be Friends with Your Children
Parenting is a balancing act, and one of the hardest parts is finding that sweet spot where you're both a guide and a friend. In my experience, children who have a friendship with their parents feel more comfortable sharing their challenges and aspirations. This is invaluable.

Too often, I've seen parents enforce a rigid structure in their relationship with their children, which can create a sense of fear. When a child is afraid of their parent, they hide things. They don't share their troubles or ask for advice. You want to be their confidant, not just their authority figure. Be a friend to your child. Laugh with them, learn with them, and most importantly, let them know they can come to you with anything.

3. Teach Them to Stand Up for Themselves
We live in a world that sometimes feels like it's dominated by passive observers. As parents, you have the power to raise

children who are leaders, not bystanders. Teach your child to stand up for themselves and others. They should be confident enough to defend their beliefs and to step in when they see someone being mistreated.

Children who know how to defend themselves grow up with a sense of self-worth and integrity. They don't shy away from challenges, and they understand that it's okay to disagree respectfully. Raise children who are strong in character and unafraid to stand for what's right. The world needs more of them.

4. Let Them Build Their Own Opinions

One of the greatest gifts you can give your child is the ability to think for themselves. Instead of dictating what they should believe, teach them how to form their own opinions. Ask questions that encourage them to explain their perspective, challenge them to consider different viewpoints, and show them how to justify their stance.

When you allow your child to think independently, you're not just raising a follower – you're raising a leader. Don't tell them what to think. Guide them on how to think. Encourage curiosity, and let them know it's okay to question things – even if that means questioning you.

5. Encourage a Love for Learning

Learning doesn't stop at the classroom door. In fact, some of the best lessons happen outside of it. Cultivate a daily habit of learning in your home. This doesn't have to mean hours of study; even 30 minutes a day can make a difference. It could be reading a book, listening to a podcast, or watching an educational video online.

Go on family trips to museums, art galleries, and science centres. These outings spark curiosity, creativity, and wonder.

Show them that learning is a lifelong journey and that knowledge is the most powerful tool they'll ever have.

MOTIVATION MULTIPLIER: HELPING STUDENTS SEE THE BIGGER PICTURE

One of the most powerful ways to keep students motivated is by helping them understand the *"why"* behind their studies. The Motivation Multiplier is a simple yet transformative concept that involves focusing on the student's ultimate goals – their *end in mind* – rather than just the immediate tasks at hand. Exams, homework, and study sessions are important, but they are merely stepping stones towards a larger purpose.

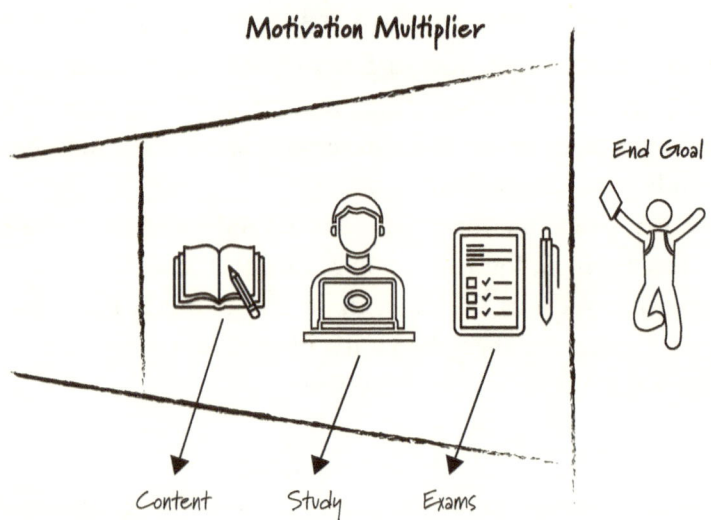

For example, a child who dreams of becoming a surgeon must excel in biology and chemistry to achieve that goal. A student aspiring to be an actor needs to develop communication and performance skills. A future professional football player must balance academics with athletic training. By tying academic work to their long-term aspirations, students see the relevance of what they're learning, making them more engaged and driven.

As parents, it's essential to encourage your child to think beyond the next test or assignment. Help them visualise their future and connect their current efforts to their dreams. This shift in mindset can dramatically enhance engagement and performance.

In fact, studies have shown that students who keep their ultimate goals in mind experience a 97% increase in engagement compared to those who focus solely on immediate academic tasks. This is the power of the Motivation Multiplier.

Practical Tips for Parents:
- **Discuss Career Goals:** Regularly talk to your child about their dreams and aspirations. What do they want to achieve in life?
- **Connect Schoolwork to Goals:** Help them understand how their current studies are a necessary step towards achieving their long-term goals.
- **Celebrate Progress:** Acknowledge their milestones along the way, reinforcing the connection between effort and future success.

By applying the Motivation Multiplier, parents can inspire their children to stay focused, work harder, and persevere through challenges, all while keeping their eyes on the prize – their dreams and future achievements.

6. Believe in Their Dreams

Your child will look to you for approval and encouragement. Believe in them, even when their dreams seem impractical or far-fetched. The truth is, our limiting beliefs often come from those closest to us. Don't let your fears or past disappointments stifle their dreams. Let them know you're behind them, no matter what.

I've seen so many parents try to live out their own unfulfilled dreams through their children. Don't place that burden on them. If you have a dream, pursue it yourself. Let your child forge their path. Encourage them to become obsessive about their passion, not yours.

7. Lead by Example

Children learn more from what we do than what we say. If you tell them to read, read yourself. If you want them to be disciplined, show them discipline in your own life. I've lost count of how many parents complain that their child is always glued to the TV, but when I ask them how they spend their evenings, they admit they're in front of the screen too.

When I was building Success Tutoring, I often worked late into the night. I wanted to show my team the importance of dedication and hard work. Similarly, as parents, you need to model the behaviours you want your children to adopt. If you want them to value education, show them that you're committed to learning too. Lead by example, and they'll follow.

8. Teach the Value of Hard Work

Hard work is one of the most valuable lessons you can impart to your child. Regardless of your family's financial situation, children should understand that nothing worth having comes easy. I remember the day I signed the lease for our first tutoring centre in Green Valley. That same day, I bought furniture and started assembling it. I worked late into the night, putting together tables and chairs.

Years later, I still see the owners of the commercial complex, worth millions, maintaining the property themselves. It taught me that wealth doesn't replace the value of hard work – it reinforces it. Teach your children to take pride in their efforts, no matter what they're working on.

9. Give Them the Freedom to Explore

Encourage your children to try different things. Extra-curricular activities aren't just a way to keep kids busy; they're a way to help them discover their passions. When a child finds their true passion, they excel beyond what anyone thought possible. Give them the chance to explore, to fail, and to try again.

10. Encourage a Growth Mindset

Language matters. If you say, "We can't afford this," or, "You can only choose one," you're teaching your child that resources are scarce and that they should limit their expectations. Instead, encourage them to think abundantly. I remember when I was starting Success Tutoring and was hesitant about buying a $100 whiteboard. My mother told me, "Buy two." That simple advice taught me to think beyond immediate limits.

Encourage your children to believe that anything is possible. A growth mindset will empower them to overcome challenges and pursue their goals with confidence.

11. Celebrate Their Achievements

Celebrate your child's achievements, big and small. Recognise their hard work and progress. When I first started tutoring, I would take my team out to a local burger place after a long week. Celebrating their efforts brought us closer and reinforced the value of perseverance.

Your child will remember the times you acknowledged their efforts. Celebrating their victories gives them the motivation to keep going, to keep pushing, and to keep dreaming.

12. Encourage Questions and Curiosity
Kids are naturally curious, but too often, their questions are brushed aside. Don't be the parent who dismisses their curiosity. Encourage them to ask questions, and if you don't know the answer, encourage them to find it themselves. There are so many resources available, from books to podcasts to videos. Teach them that every question is worth exploring.

13. Choose the Right Tutoring Provider
Tutoring can play a crucial role in a child's academic journey. It's an incredible tool for helping students overcome challenges, develop confidence, and discover a love for learning. However, with so many options available, choosing the right tutoring provider is essential.

Look for a provider whose values align with yours. Success Tutoring, for example, emphasises motivation, inspiration, and personal growth alongside academic excellence. In today's world, academics alone aren't enough. Students need to develop resilience, confidence, and a sense of purpose. A provider that prioritises these qualities will ensure your child isn't just learning but growing as a person.

Many tutoring centres are solely focused on academic performance, but that's only part of the picture. You want a place where your child will feel encouraged, valued, and understood. The right environment can transform tutoring from a chore into a journey of discovery. Find a provider that sees your child as more than a grade and focuses on their overall development. Remember, education isn't just about what they learn; it's about who they become along the way.

As parents, you have the power to inspire, to guide, and to instill values that will carry your children through life. Each of these tips is a small step, but taken together, they create a foundation for a fulfilled, confident, and resilient individual.

Parenting isn't about being perfect; it's about being present, being real, and being willing to learn alongside your child. Take these tips to heart, and remember that the most important thing you can do for your child is to believe in them and show them how to believe in themselves.

CHAPTER 22

TIPS FOR POTENTIAL FRANCHISE PARTNERS

Becoming a franchise partner is a powerful way to step into the world of business ownership while leveraging a proven model and established brand. However, it's essential to approach this journey with the right mindset and strategies. This chapter is dedicated to those of you who are considering taking the leap into franchising. I've gathered insights and lessons from my own experience with Success Tutoring, which I hope will serve as a roadmap as you explore the possibilities of becoming a franchise partner.

1. Pick the Right Industry
First and foremost, choose an industry you're passionate about. This can't be emphasised enough. When you're in business for yourself, every single day will involve challenges that test your resolve. If you're not deeply invested in the industry, those challenges can quickly become overwhelming. If you love what you do, those same challenges become opportunities for growth, learning, and development.

For example, I've always had a passion for education and helping others reach their full potential. When I founded Success Tutoring, I was driven by a mission to motivate, inspire, and uplift students. I genuinely believe that the right tutor can change a student's life. Every franchise partner who joins Success Tutoring shares this same passion for education and making a difference. Find a franchise opportunity that excites you, because passion is the fuel that will keep you moving forwards, even on the tough days.

2. Pick the Right Franchise
Once you've chosen your industry, it's crucial to find a franchise that aligns with your personal values. Every franchise has a unique culture and philosophy, and it's essential to select a company that resonates with you on a fundamental level. Ask yourself: does this franchise have the same commitment to quality, integrity, and service that I do? Does its mission align with my own beliefs and goals?

I remember speaking with one of our franchise partners who had previously worked in various industries. He explained that when he came across Success Tutoring, he felt an immediate connection to our mission and values. He saw the dedication we had towards empowering young minds, and he knew it was the right fit for him. It's important to choose a franchise you can genuinely believe in and support wholeheartedly. If you don't feel a connection to the brand's core values, it may not be the right choice for you.

FRANCHISE FIT TEST: A SELF-EVALUATION TOOL FOR PROSPECTIVE FRANCHISEES

Owning a tutoring franchise is a rewarding journey, but it requires the right mindset, skills, and financial readiness. The Success Tutoring Franchise Fit Test is a practical self-evaluation tool designed to help prospective franchise partners assess their readiness for this life-changing opportunity. By answering key questions and scoring themselves across various dimensions, individuals can identify their strengths, weaknesses, and overall fit for the Success Tutoring model.

How the Franchise Fit Test Works
The test covers five critical dimensions that are essential for franchise success:
1. **Passion Alignment:** Are you passionate about motivating and uplifting students?
2. **Business Mindset:** Do you have the resilience and problem-solving skills to run a business?
3. **Financial Readiness:** Are you financially prepared to invest and sustain the business during the early stages?
4. **Leadership Skills:** Can you effectively lead a team and build a community presence?
5. **System Compatibility:** Are you willing to follow established systems and processes?

FRANCHISE FIT TEST TABLE

Dimension	Key Questions	Score (1-5)
1. Passion Alignment	I am passionate about motivating and uplifting students.	
	I am genuinely interested in education and personal development.	
	I believe in Success Tutoring's mission and philosophy.	
Subtotal (Out of 15):		

MILLIONAIRE TUTOR

Dimension	Key Questions	Score (1-5)
2. Business Mindset	I enjoy solving problems and thrive in challenging situations.	
	I am resilient and can bounce back from setbacks.	
	I am open to learning new skills and adapting to change.	
Subtotal (Out of 15):		
3. Financial Readiness	I have the required capital to invest in the franchise and cover initial costs.	
	I have a financial safety net to support myself during the first 6–12 months of operation.	
	I am comfortable reinvesting in my business for marketing and growth.	
Subtotal (Out of 15):		
4. Leadership Skills	I have experience leading or managing a team effectively.	
	I can inspire and motivate others to deliver excellent results.	
	I am comfortable networking and promoting my business in the community.	
Subtotal (Out of 15):		
5. System Compatibility	I am willing to follow established systems and processes for consistency.	
	I value branding and understand the importance of maintaining high standards.	
	I am coachable and open to constructive feedback.	
Subtotal (Out of 15):		

For each question, rate yourself on a scale of 1 to 5:
- **1:** Strongly Disagree
- **2:** Disagree
- **3:** Neutral
- **4:** Agree
- **5:** Strongly Agree

Add up your scores for each section to calculate your total fit score. Use the scoring guide to interpret your results.

Scoring Guide
- **60–75:** Excellent Fit – You're well-prepared to succeed as a franchisee.
- **45–59:** Moderate Fit – You have potential but may need to address certain areas.
- **Below 45:** Needs Improvement – Consider addressing gaps before moving forwards.

Taking the time to complete the Franchise Fit Test helps prospective franchisees make informed decisions about their future. It encourages reflection on key areas such as passion, resilience, financial readiness, leadership, and compatibility with Success Tutoring's systems. By understanding where they stand, individuals can take proactive steps to strengthen their readiness, increasing their chances of long-term success.

Remember, as Jim Collins said, *"Great vision without great people is irrelevant."* The Franchise Fit Test ensures that the right people are joining the Success Tutoring family – those who are truly ready to make a positive impact in their communities.

3. Do your numbers

Before signing any franchise agreement, it's crucial that prospective franchisees take the time to *do their numbers*. This means thoroughly assessing the financial aspects of the business to ensure it aligns with their personal goals and lifestyle needs. Understanding initial investment costs, operational expenses, projected revenues, and profit margins is essential to making an informed decision.

INCOME REPLACEMENT CALCULATOR

One of the biggest questions potential franchise partners ask is, *"How do I know when it's the right time to leave my corporate job?"* The Income Replacement Calculator is a practical tool designed to answer that question by providing a clear roadmap for achieving financial independence through a tutoring franchise. This step-by-step framework helps prospective franchisees calculate how much revenue their tutoring centre needs to generate to replace one or both partners' corporate incomes.

The calculator simplifies financial planning into five key steps:

Step 1: Define Your Target Income

Start by determining how much income your household needs to maintain your current lifestyle. Calculate your combined household income and divide it into monthly targets.

Example:
- Current household income: $200,000/year.
- Necessary monthly income: $16,667.
- Add a savings goal: $3,000/month.
- **Target monthly income:** $19,667.

Step 2: Calculate Franchise Revenue Needs

Next, calculate how much revenue your tutoring centre needs to cover both operational costs and your target income.

Example:
- Monthly operational costs: $14,000.
- Profit margin: 40%.
- **Target revenue:** ($19,667 + $14,000) ÷ 0.40 = $84,167 month.

Step 3: Translate Revenue Into Student Enrolment
Determine how many students you need to enrol to meet your revenue goals.

Example:
- Average monthly fee per student: $300.
- **Target student enrolment:** $84,167 ÷ $300 = 281 students.

Step 4: Create a Phased Growth Plan
Break down your journey into achievable phases:
- **Phase 1:** Breakeven stage with 100 students.
- **Phase 2:** Scale-up stage with 200 students.
- **Phase 3:** Full income replacement with 281 students.

Step 5: Plan for Scaling
Once your first centre reaches capacity, explore opening a second location to double your potential income.

Example:
- Two sites with 281 students each = $168,600/month revenue.
- This far exceeds the original $200,000 household income target.

The Income Replacement Calculator provides clarity and confidence by breaking big financial goals into manageable steps. It's realistic, actionable, and customisable to fit each franchise partner's unique situation. Most importantly, it shows that replacing your corporate income isn't just a dream – it's a tangible, achievable goal.

4. Learn from Other Franchise Partners

One of the greatest advantages of joining a franchise network is the community of like-minded business owners you'll become a part of. The network provides an invaluable opportunity to share insights, learn from one another, and collaborate. In many ways, your fellow franchise partners are one of your best resources for success. They've been where you are, and they understand the unique challenges and rewards of running the same business.

Within Success Tutoring, I've seen countless examples of franchise partners connecting with one another, sharing marketing tips, discussing local challenges, and even brainstorming solutions together. Each partner brings a unique perspective, and collectively, they make the entire network stronger. Don't be afraid to reach out, ask questions, and learn from those around you. In a franchise, success isn't just an individual journey – it's a shared one.

5. Work Hard and Market Locally

While the franchisor will provide you with a framework, the success of your business is ultimately in your hands. This means putting in the effort to market locally and build relationships within your community. Attend local events, sponsor community activities, and get involved. By becoming a visible and valued member of your community, you'll build a loyal customer base and strengthen your reputation.

When I started Success Tutoring, I tried every marketing method under the sun. I put up posters, distributed flyers, and held free workshops. Some of these methods worked better than others, but what always made the biggest impact was word of mouth. Focus on delivering exceptional service to your customers, and they'll become your best marketers. Remember, local marketing and building relationships are key components of growing a successful franchise.

6. Don't Get Too Arrogant

There's a famous quote I love: "Pride comes before a fall." Success in franchising requires a combination of humility and confidence. Yes, believe in yourself, but avoid the trap of thinking you know it all. One of the most common mistakes I've seen franchise partners make is assuming they don't need to follow the system or listen to advice because they think they know better. It's easy to become overconfident, but remember that arrogance can quickly lead to mistakes and setbacks.

Stay open to feedback, remain teachable, and remember that there's always more to learn. The most successful franchise partners are those who combine confidence with humility. They're willing to follow the system, accept constructive criticism, and continue growing both personally and professionally.

7. Focus on Your Customers

At the end of the day, your customers are the foundation of your business. When I was first building Success Tutoring, I experimented with all sorts of marketing tactics. Some worked, others didn't, but the one thing that consistently brought results was focusing on the customers. When you prioritise delivering value and achieving results for your clients, your business will grow naturally through word of mouth.

If you focus on your customers' needs, they'll become your biggest advocates. They'll refer their friends and family, leave positive reviews, and support your business in countless ways. As a franchise partner, your success will ultimately depend on your ability to provide outstanding service to each and every customer.

8. Provide Feedback – but Follow Decisions

In a franchise system, feedback is essential. We rely on our franchise partners to share their experiences, insights, and suggestions. However, it's also crucial to understand that once a decision is made, the entire network needs to move in the same direction. There's a quote that captures this perfectly: "There is always time for discussion about different opinions and ideas; however, when a decision is made, we are all steering in the same direction."

Your feedback is valued and important, but once the franchisor makes a final decision, it's essential to follow it. This consistency is what makes a franchise successful. By maintaining uniformity and standardisation, we ensure that customers receive the same high-quality experience across all locations. Remember, a franchise is a team effort, and for it to work, everyone needs to row in unison.

9. Be Ready to Learn

Starting a franchise may be easier than building a business from scratch, but that doesn't mean it's easy. There's still a lot to learn, and as a franchise partner, you'll need to invest time and effort into understanding the system, mastering the processes, and continually improving your skills.

One of the biggest benefits of franchising is the training and support you'll receive from the franchisor. Take full advantage of this. Attend training sessions, participate in workshops, and never stop learning. In business, there's always room for growth, and the more you learn, the more successful you'll become.

10. Leverage the Brand's Recognition
One of the primary advantages of joining a franchise is the brand recognition that comes with it. In the case of Success Tutoring, we've been recognised as a leader in the tutoring industry. I've been featured on national television, including *The Today Show* and Channel 7 News. These appearances build credibility, and as a franchise partner, you should use this brand recognition to your advantage.

When speaking with potential clients, highlight the brand's achievements. Share the success stories, and let people know that they're choosing a business that has been proven to deliver results. Leverage the brand's reputation to build trust and confidence with your customers. Remember, you're part of a larger story, and you can use that to strengthen your own marketing efforts.

Becoming a franchise partner is an exciting and rewarding journey. It offers the opportunity to build a business with the support of a proven system, an established brand, and a network of fellow entrepreneurs. However, success in franchising requires the right mindset, a commitment to the system, and a genuine passion for the work.

If you're ready to take the leap, remember these tips. Choose an industry and a franchise that aligns with your values, be willing to learn, stay focused on your customers, and never stop growing. With dedication, hard work, and the support of the franchise network, you'll be well on your way to building a thriving business.

CHAPTER 23

TIPS FOR ASPIRING FRANCHISORS

Over the years, as I've grown Success Tutoring from a small, single-centre business to a franchised brand, I've gathered a wealth of knowledge on what it truly takes to build and scale a franchise. It's been a journey filled with milestones, tough decisions, and invaluable lessons. I want to share my top tips for those of you considering franchising your own business. These aren't just strategies – they're philosophies that have shaped my path as an entrepreneur.

1. Think Big
When I first considered franchising Success Tutoring, I knew I had to start thinking on a larger scale. This business began in a spare room in Western Sydney, a long way from the polished skyscrapers of Sydney's CBD. But when I committed to franchising, I knew I needed to build an environment that reflected my vision. I took a big step by leasing a serviced office in Barangaroo, a premier location in Sydney. The office had one of the best views in Australia, overlooking the harbor

and the iconic Opera House. It was a significant investment, but it was also a mindset shift. Moving from a small, hidden space in Western Sydney to a major business district was a signal that we were ready to grow.

The decision was risky, and I remember being on the train, signing the lease and paying the deposit on the way to a meeting with a major potential partner. The meeting was a success, and we gained confidence in what we were building. If you're serious about franchising, build your brand in a way that reflects where you want to go, not where you are now. I remember telling my team (Cassidy A, Timothy N and Jason K), "We've come this far. We must never forget our roots and where we came from, but we must keep our focus on the bigger picture".

2. Try Everything

When I started, I left no stone unturned. I used every marketing technique I could think of to get the word out about Success Tutoring. I printed posters, distributed flyers, and even asked local businesses if they'd display our information. Sometimes I'd spend early mornings putting up posters around the neighbourhood, advertising Success Tutoring as "The Best Tutor" on street poles, bus stops, and bulletin boards.

In the early days, I also invested in a tech team to build a custom software for us, spending over $30,000 on a project that we never even ended up using. I learned an important lesson: sometimes things don't work out as planned, but that's okay. The key is to be willing to pivot, try different approaches, and keep moving forwards. Not everything will stick, but every experiment will bring you one step closer to what does work. Don't be afraid to try things, especially when you're starting out. You'll find that even failures bring valuable insights.

3. Focus on the Business, Not Just the Franchise

One thing I learned quickly was that franchising is a by-product of building a strong business foundation. If your business model doesn't work well, franchising it won't suddenly fix it. You need to focus on the core business and make sure it's running like a well-oiled machine before even thinking about franchising.

When I started franchising, I spent a lot of time improving the business operations, processes, and customer experience. Results sell far better than ideas. Before you approach potential franchise partners, make sure your business is in top shape, with consistent results and a model that's easy to replicate. It's one thing to sell a concept, but it's far more effective to sell a proven system.

4. Surround Yourself with the Right Coaches

You'll find "coaches" for just about everything, but choose wisely. Seek advice from people who have actually done what you're trying to do. I never reached out to someone I admired who didn't respond or wasn't willing to help. If they're where you want to be, reach out, learn from them, and take their advice to heart.

I learned from those who had built successful franchises, and their insights were invaluable. Franchising isn't something you should try to figure out alone. Surround yourself with mentors who have walked the path before you. They'll help you navigate the inevitable challenges, avoid costly mistakes, and provide insights you won't find anywhere else.

5. Follow Your Intuition

Your intuition is a powerful tool. In my experience, the best decisions often come from following that inner voice. If you're in tune with yourself and aligned with a higher purpose, you'll find success. I've seen a strong connection between people who achieve big things and those who believe in something greater than themselves.

There were times when I didn't have all the information or felt uncertain, but I followed my intuition, and it led me in the right direction. Trust that inner guidance, especially when making big decisions. When you're in tune with your purpose and focused on the long-term impact, you'll naturally gravitate towards the right choices.

6. Prioritise Your Franchise Partners

Franchising changes your focus from directly serving customers to serving your franchise partners. They become your customers. Your job is to make their experience as seamless as possible and to set them up for success. I had the opportunity to learn from Jim Penman, the founder of Jim's Group, one of the largest franchisors in Australia. He shared three core principles that stuck with me:
- Your first priority should always be the welfare of your franchise partners.
- Stay passionate about customer service.
- Only partner with franchise partners and franchisors that you are convinced will succeed.

By focusing on your franchise partners, you create a culture of trust and support. Franchise partners need to feel like they're part of something bigger, a network that genuinely cares about their success. Build a system that provides them with the resources, support, and encouragement they need.

7. Be Prepared to Make Tough Decisions

Franchising is a demanding journey, and it will test you in ways you never expected. You'll need to make hard decisions, like hiring and firing staff, re-evaluating your strategy, and standing firm on what you believe in. It's not for the faint of heart, but if you're committed, it's incredibly rewarding.

Running a franchise organisation requires perseverance, dedication, and resilience. Remember, if it were easy, everyone would do it. Be prepared to make sacrifices and take the hard road when necessary. It's all part of building something lasting.

8. Work-Life Balance Does Not Exist

As a franchisor, you can forget about work-life balance, at least in the beginning. You'll need to pour everything you have into building a strong foundation for your franchise system. That might mean working long hours, making personal sacrifices, and putting your business ahead of everything else.

While balance may seem ideal, remember that growth requires a season of sacrifice. When you're committed to building something bigger than yourself, work-life balance becomes less relevant. Dedicate yourself to the business, and don't expect it to be easy.

9. Public Relations and Branding

Building a strong brand is essential for scaling your franchise network. A well-crafted brand story can propel your business to new heights. As the founder, your personal story is an extension of the brand. Leverage it, share it, and use it to inspire others.

A strong personal brand can open doors, attract franchise partners, and establish your credibility. Invest time in developing your public relations strategy, and don't shy away from the spotlight. Your story will resonate with people, and they'll feel a connection to what you're building.

10. Reinvest Everything Back into the Business

Never have a Plan B. Only have one plan, and that's to succeed. Reinvest every dollar back into the business, especially in the early stages. It might mean living frugally or making personal sacrifices, but that's what it takes to build something meaningful.

I've always been a firm believer in going all-in. If you truly believe in what you're building, put everything you have into it. There's no room for a backup plan. When you commit 100%, you'll push through obstacles and find ways to make it work.

11. Consider a Strategic Partnership

If you're serious about scaling your franchise, consider partnering with others who can help you achieve your vision. I recently started the Black Franchise Group (BFG) to assist aspiring franchisors in building and scaling their businesses. We invest heavily in these businesses and guide them through every step of the franchising process.

A strategic partner can bring resources, expertise, and connections that will accelerate your growth. It's a powerful way to scale your business while sharing the journey with like-minded individuals.

Franchising is a challenging yet incredibly fulfilling journey. It requires dedication, resilience, and a commitment to continuous improvement. If you're ready to think big, try everything, and prioritise the success of your franchise partners, you'll be well on your way to building something extraordinary. Remember, every step you take in this journey is an investment in the future, not just for you but for everyone who joins you. So take that leap, keep learning, and never lose sight of your vision.

CHAPTER 24

10 YEARS OF KNOWLEDGE IN ONE CHAPTER

When I look back at my journey over the last decade, it's clear that the path was not always smooth. There were hurdles, setbacks, and moments I genuinely felt like giving up. But one thing I've come to understand is this: perseverance is power. I'm here today because I didn't let those moments of doubt dictate my future. And if there's one thing I want you to take away from this chapter, it's that the journey to success is often paved with relentless perseverance, self-belief, and learning from every experience.

LESSONS LEARNED ALONG THE WAY

Over the years, I've gathered a few core lessons that I believe are the bedrock of any successful venture. Let's dive into those.

1. **Have a Vision Board:** Your vision board is a powerful tool. It's not just a collage of images but a roadmap for your dreams. When I was starting out, I crafted a vision board that reflected my goals and the life I wanted to build.

For instance, if you aspire to build a successful business, put up images of businesses or entrepreneurs who inspire you. This will bring clarity and direction to your life. Your vision board should be something you look at every day; let it remind you of what you're working towards.

2. **Keep Friendships and Business Separate:** Early on, I made the mistake of intertwining friendships with business. It's completely fine to hire friends, especially when you're just starting, but always keep a balance between friendship and professionalism. I've had friends in the business, and while it made the work environment fun, it also blurred the lines. Make it clear that professionalism is non-negotiable, even if you're close outside of work.

3. **Plan Your Expenses Carefully:** Regardless of how much you make, poor financial planning can lead to serious trouble. One of the earliest lessons I learned was to always question whether every cent I spent was bringing back value to the business. Always track your expenses meticulously and ensure that your investments are driving growth. Your expenses are not just numbers; they're reflections of your priorities. Let every dollar you spend be purposeful.

4. **Be Prepared to Lose Friends:** As you evolve, your mindset and goals will change, and you may find that people around you aren't on the same journey. This is normal, but it can be hard. Over time, you'll find yourself gravitating towards people who uplift you rather than drag you down. Cherish those who stick by you and let go of the ones who don't align with your vision. You're only as strong as the people you surround yourself with, so choose wisely.

5. **Dedicate Yourself to Lifelong Learning:** Stay hungry to learn. Whether it's reading, watching educational

content, or even talking to people in different fields, never stop learning. Every bit of knowledge is a stepping stone towards where you want to be. And remember, growth isn't just about learning things in your industry; it's about broadening your perspective in all areas of life.

6. **Never Give Up on Your Dreams:** If you never give up, you never truly fail. Failure only occurs when you stop trying. I remember feeling overwhelmed at the end of 2022, so much so that I almost threw in the towel. I sent a message to Doug that read:

> *"Hi Doug, Hope you are well. I'm coming very close to leaving the tutoring business and starting something new…I feel like I'm putting too much work into something that isn't resulting in equal or more reward."*

But here I am, still standing. I didn't give up, and that's why I'm still here. Don't let a rough patch dictate the end of your story. There is always another chapter waiting to be written.

CORE BUSINESS PHILOSOPHIES

My business philosophy can be broken down into a few principles that guide everything I do:

- **Give Before You Receive**
  In business, giving value should come first. I've found that when you focus on providing value to others, the rewards follow naturally. Build a business that genuinely helps others, and you'll find that success will follow.
- **Honesty Above All**
  Running a business isn't just about making money. It's about being genuine, building trust, and creating a culture of honesty. I've always believed that honesty is the best way to lead a team and build strong client relationships.

- **Execution Over Ideas**
  An idea without execution is worthless. You need a strong team to bring those ideas to life. I've seen people get fixated on coming up with the "next big idea," but here's the truth: ideas are great, but it's the execution that wins.

THE PIVOTAL MOMENTS

I've made mistakes, and I've faced setbacks. But each of these experiences taught me invaluable lessons.

One time, I made the mistake of helping prospective franchise partners by securing a location and handling council approvals before they'd signed the franchise agreement. In the end, they decided not to proceed with the franchise and copied the business model for themselves. This was a tough lesson, but it taught me the importance of protecting your processes. I now ensure that all agreements are signed before moving forwards.

Another major turning point was when I realised that I needed strong advisors and experts around me. During COVID-19, an accountant advised me to apply for a government grant, which later resulted in complications. I ultimately learned that, as a business owner, I am responsible for every decision, and it's crucial to have the right advisors. You don't delegate responsibility – only tasks.

PERSONAL GROWTH AND SELF-AWARENESS

A business can only grow as much as its founder is willing to grow. Over the years, I've pushed myself to constantly learn, research, and expand my skill set. Whether it was signing a commercial lease for the first time or diving into the world of franchising, I embraced every learning curve. As the leader, you need to be aware of what you don't know and have a hunger to fill those gaps.

When times were tough, I found solace in small rituals. One of my favourites was waking up early to drive to Bondi Beach for a morning jog. Watching the sunrise over the ocean gave me clarity and motivation. Find your happy place and lean on it when you need a moment of peace and reflection.

KEY ADVICE FOR ASPIRING ENTREPRENEURS

- **Create a Vision Board**
  Keep your goals visible. It's a daily reminder of where you're headed and why you started in the first place.
- **Build a Network of Supportive People**
  Surround yourself with individuals who uplift you. You're the average of the five people you spend the most time with, so choose carefully.
- **Focus on Execution**
  As much as planning and brainstorming are essential, nothing replaces action. Get out there, make mistakes, and learn as you go.
- **Believe in Yourself**
  Self-belief is the foundation of success. There will be times when it feels like you're the only one who believes in your vision, and that's okay. If you're willing to put in the work, your belief will pay off.

BUILDING THE MINDSET FOR SUCCESS

The right mindset can be the difference between success and failure. I encourage you to develop an abundance mindset – one that embraces opportunity and rejects limitations. I've seen this in practice with some of my top-performing franchise partners, who are willing to take risks, like selling their homes to open more Success Tutoring locations. That's the kind of dedication that drives success. They understand that it's not just about the comfort of owning a home but about creating a thriving business that can offer even greater rewards.

LESSONS FROM THE LAST 10 YEARS

The journey hasn't been easy, but it has been worth every moment. Over the years, I've seen that consistent effort, resilience, and an unwavering belief in your purpose will carry you further than you can imagine. Your journey is yours to shape, so take charge, be relentless, and don't settle until you've achieved what you set out to accomplish.

In the end, the knowledge I've shared here is a culmination of countless lessons, hard work, and a lot of trial and error. If you can take just one thing from this chapter, let it be this: keep throwing until it sticks. Never stop moving, learning, and pushing forwards, because every step you take is a step closer to achieving your dreams.

www.ingramcontent.com/pod-product-compliance
Lightning Source LLC
Chambersburg PA
CBHW030317080526
44584CB00012B/603